Collins · do brilliantly!

Ins... G...

The ... here

Andrew Bennett
Keith Brindle
Series Editor: Jayne de Courcy

Published by HarperCollins*Publishers* Ltd
77–85 Fulham Palace Road
London W6 8JB

www.**Collins**Education.com
On-line support for schools and colleges

First published 2001
This revised edition published 2004
10 9 8 7 6 5 4 3
ISBN 0 00 717258 3

British Library Cataloguing in Publication Data
A catalogue record for this book is available from the British Library.

Edited by Steve Attmore, Sue Chapple and Jenny Draine
Production by Katie Butler
Original design by Gecko Ltd
This edition designed by Bob Vickers
Cover design by Susi Martin-Taylor
Illustrations by Chris Rothero, Gecko Ltd and John Plumb
Printed and bound by Printing Express, Hong Kong

Contents

Acknowledgements

The Authors and Publishers are grateful to the following for permission to reproduce extracts from copyright material:

A *Kestrel for a Knave* by Barry Hines (Michael Joseph, 1968), reproduced by permission of Penguin Books Ltd (pp 71 and 77); *And when did you last see your father?* by Blake Morrison by permission of The Peter Fraser & Dunlop Group Ltd (pp 29 and 73); 'Badger's Rampage' article by Rod Chaytor for *The Daily Mirror* (p 3); 'Escape for head who allowed cheating' article by Becky Sharpe for the TES (p 32); 'Even Tho', reproduced with permission from Curtis Brown Ltd, London, on behalf of Grace Nichols © Grace Nichols 1989 (p 53); George Adamson (article) from the TES (p 95); *Going Solo* by Roald Dahl, reprinted by permission of David Higham Associates (pp 28 and 77); Health Education Authority (poster) (p 23); *Hong Kong* by permission of A P Watt Ltd on behalf of Jan Morris (p 72); 'Hypnotising the Cat' by Mike Harding (p 92); 'I Am Very Bothered' by Simon Armitage published by Faber & Faber Ltd (p 39); 'Jac Codi Baw' by Gillian Clarke, published by Carcanet Press Limited (p 39); 'Life Doesn't Frighten Me' by Maya Angelou from *And Still I Rise*, published by Random House Publishers (p 41); *Lord of the Flies* by William Golding, published by Faber & Faber Ltd (pp 63, 64 and 71); Metro News (article) (p 91); 'Mid-term break' by Seamus Heaney published by Faber & Faber Ltd (p 37); National Westminster Bank plc (advert) (p 91); 'Night of the Scorpion' by Nissim Ezekiel in *Latter Day Psalms*, reprinted by permission of Oxford University Press, New Delhi (pp 39, 46 and 52); *Notes from a Small Island* © Bill Bryson 1995, published by Black Swan, a division of Transworld Publishers Ltd. All rights reserved (pp 28 and 69); 'Poem at Thirty-Nine' from *Horses Make a Landscape More Beautiful* by Alice Walker, published in Great Britain by The Women's Press Ltd, 1985, 34 Great Sutton Street, London EC1V 0DX, used by permission of David Higham Associates (p 40); Privilege Insurance (advert) (The Royal Bank of Scotland) (p 11); RSPCA (advert) (p 33); *Salt on the Snow* by Rukshana Smith, published by Bodley Head and used by permission of The Random House Group Limited (p 66); *The Daily Mail* (article) (p 113); 'The Darkness Out There' from Penelope Lively's *Pack of Cards and Other Stories*, published by Faber & Faber Ltd (pp 65, 66, 69 and 76); 'The Early Purges' by Seamus Heaney published by Faber & Faber Ltd (p 40); *The Guardian* (article) (p 109); *The Kingdom by the Sea* by Paul Theroux, published by Penguin Books (p 7); *The Observer* (article) (p 92); 'The Outing: A Story' in a *Dylan Thomas Treasury*, reprinted by permission of David Higham Associates (p 72); *The Subtle Knife* by Philip Pullman (p 105); 'Thistles' from *Wodwo* by Ted Hughes, published by Faber & Faber Ltd (p 36); 'Turned' by Charlotte Perkins Gilman from the *Charlotte Gilman Reader* edited by Anne Lane, published in Great Britain by The Women's Press Ltd, 1985, 34 Great Sutton Street, London EC1V 0DX used by permission of The Women's Press Ltd (pp 65, 66 and 76); *What Car?* (May 1998) published by Haymarket Motoring Publications Ltd (p 21); 'When the teacher knew best' article by Simon Jenkins for *The Yorkshire Evening Post* (p 32); 'Wil Williams' (1861–1910) by Gillian Clarke, published by Carcanet Press Limited (p 69); **www.bbc.co.uk** for the website page (p 33)

Photographs and illustrations

BFI Stills/Canal & Image UK (pp 61 and 80); Chris Rothero; Colin Seddon/Naturepl.com (p 4); Gecko Ltd; John Plumb

Every effort has been made to contact the holders of copyright material. If any have been inadvertently overlooked, the Publishers will be pleased to make the necessary arrangements at the first opportunity.

Get the most out of your

Instant Revision pocket book

1 **Maximise your revision time.** You can carry this book around with you anywhere. This means you can spend any spare moments dipping into it.

2 **Learn and remember what you need to know.** This book contains all the really important things you need to know for your exam. All the information is set out clearly and concisely, making it easy for you to revise.

3 **Find out what you don't know.** The *Check yourself* questions and *Score chart* help you to see quickly and easily the topics you're good at and those you're not so good at.

What's in this book?

1 *The skills* – just what you need to know

Reading and Writing

- There are sections covering important reading and writing topics that you will need in your GCSE English exam.
- The authors use carefully chosen examples from fiction and non-fiction texts to show you how to improve your skills, as well as the work of examination candidates.

Exam guidance

- This book shows you how to prepare for your exams and how to tackle exam questions.

2 *Check yourself* questions – find out how much you know and boost your grade

- Each *Check yourself* is linked to one or more skills page. The numbers after the topic heading in the *Check yourself* tell you which skills page the *Check yourself* is linked to.
- The questions ask you to demonstrate the types of skills you will need to use in the exams. They will show you what you are good at and what you need to improve on.
- The reverse side of each *Check yourself* gives you the answers **plus** tutorial help and guidance to boost your exam grade.
- There are points for each question. The total number of points for each *Check yourself* is always 20. When you check your answers, fill in the score box alongside each answer with the number of points you feel you scored.

3 The *Score chart* – an instant picture of your strengths and weaknesses

- *Score chart (1)* lists all the *Check yourself* pages.
- As you complete each *Check yourself*, record your points on the *Score chart*. This will show you instantly which areas you need to spend more time on.
- *Score chart (2)* is a graph which lets you plot your points against GCSE grades. This will give you a rough idea of how you are doing in each area. Of course, this is only a rough idea because the questions aren't real exam questions!

Use this Instant Revision pocket book on your own – or revise with a friend or relative. See who can get the highest score!

Media texts (1)

You may be asked questions about previously unseen media texts or pre-release media texts. These could include magazine and newspaper articles, reports, columns and features; advertisements and cartoons; and any text taken from the mass media.

You need to respond to the texts by explaining **how** effects are achieved, rather than just describing what is there.

In many instances, these explanations will relate to the **purpose and target audience** of the text.

Audience

Many media texts are aimed at broad groups of people, categorised by income, profession or interests. Particular advertisements, for example, will be aimed at different groups and will therefore be presented and distributed differently. Rolls Royce cars are not advertised on prime-time commercial television, but Skodas are. This allows the authors of media texts to make certain assumptions about the audience's beliefs, lifestyles and aspirations. For example, an article in a magazine for members of the National Farmers' Union begins:

> British food is clearly the best, and how to prove it beyond doubt to supermarkets, caterers and the general public, is the aim of a new industry-wide farm standards initiative being promoted by NFU.

This is neither a lively nor balanced presentation of views. The writer is addressing an audience assumed to be both interested and sympathetic.

Purpose

The purpose of a text involves what it is – an article or web page, for example – and what its aim is – why it has been written. Sometimes the aim will be to sell a product or to interest a particular group of people. In either case, the purpose is closely related to the audience. Often, audiences are seen in stereotypical terms, so cars and sport might be used to attract men, whilst fashion, food and children might be used in texts wishing to target women.

Media texts (2)

A tabloid newspaper shows a picture of Gianfranco Zola, an Italian footballer who played for Chelsea, serving a pizza under the headline:

which contains the puns typical of the medium, and is presumably intended to give fans a light-hearted view of the player. It does, of course, present a stereotypical view of Italians. Broadsheet newspapers use similar approaches, as in this headline from *The Independent*: 'FRENCH SAY NON TO LE BUSINESS SPEAK ANGLAIS'. This is designed to capture the interest of an educated readership. It also sustains the supposed hostility between the French and the English.

Media language

Media texts are often short and snappy. They are designed to **grab the reader's attention**. You should therefore look out for, and comment on, language which:

- tries to influence your opinion (e.g. 'clearly' in the NFU article)
- sounds memorable, but has no real meaning (e.g. 'Mr Muscle loves the jobs you hate')
- is partly truthful (e.g. 'kills all *known* germs')
- appeals to snobbery or fear (e.g. words such as 'exclusive'), or mentions of 'understains' in washing powder advertisements.

Structural and presentational devices

Media texts use titles, subheadings, columns, text boxes, frames, colour, varieties of fonts and illustrations to catch and direct the reader's interest.

Although questions on media texts will often focus on purpose and audience, language and presentational devices, they might also involve an analysis of **fact and opinion**, how an **argument** is put together and **comparison**.

This report from *The Daily Mirror* has been written for the general reader. It is a short item and so relies on what actually happened. Note the:

- short paragraphs
- dramatic headline
- emphasis on the celebrity who was injured
- relatively simple vocabulary
- long quotation, giving a 'personal' feel
- largely factual basis for what is said.

Arguably, all these features will appeal to the target audience: an 'everyday' reader who wants to learn what happened but is not likely to spend long on the story.

BADGER'S RAMPAGE

5 hurt by escaped pet Boris

By ROD CHAYTOR

A BADGER attacked five people including an ex-TV wildlife presenter in a 48 hour rampage after escaping from a wildlife park.

Michael Fitzgerald, 67, had to have two skin grafts after tame Boris, who had been reared as a pet, went for him in his garden.

The former Countryfile presenter went to investigate after hearing a banging against his garage door. He said: "Instead of running away, it came straight towards me, which I thought strange.

"But then it went for me and bit my arm and took a big chunk out.

"It was absolute agony. I managed to get it off and went into the house. But the badger followed and bit me on the leg. I only escaped when I managed to pick it up and throw it out."

Michael, from Evesham, Worcs, was taken to hospital by ambulance.

Boris, who got out of nearby Vale Wildlife Rescue centre, then attacked four others including a man walking home from the pub. Two policemen sent to catch him climbed on to their car bonnet to escape.

Boris was eventually caught and put down.

Animal experts said it is very unusual for a badger to attack humans.

SAVAGE: Badger attacked Michael

r.chaytor@mirror.co.uk

Fact and opinion

The opinion that the badger went on a 'rampage' is supported by facts in the report. There are details of the people attacked, the length of the incident and even medical information about Michael Fitzgerald. When he recounts the facts of the badger's attack, and we learn of policemen having to climb on their car to escape, we are convinced the animal had to be put down. The final opinion by 'animal experts' can seem anti-climactic; or, make the whole event seem even more startling.

Argument

The way the details are presented makes the badger seem aggressive and dangerous. The report opens with vivid details, brings to life what the badger did, and moves to what therefore seems a logical conclusion, with the badger destroyed.

Environment | Habitat | Food | Threats | History | Nature links

Badger friends – the site that loves badgers

Join our group: start helping badgers TODAY!

Protecting
badgers
dolphins
foxes
whales
lions
monkeys
elephants

The long white nose… the furry shape… the wandering plod… the badger in the wild. With its distinctive striped head, our friend the badger lives in woodlands, mountains and roadsides all around the UK. Of course, badgers look cute – and they are. But they have problems and **Badger friends** is a group that has been set up to help them.

Why do we need you? Well, we need your help and your financial donations to make sure our black and white friends can continue to prosper. If you can spare just a little money – or, perhaps, a little of your time – we can give our British badgers a happy future.

The Badgers Act 1992 gave legal protection to badgers and their setts, and it is now an offence to disturb or ill-treat them. Yet these shy creatures are still far from safe. And that is where **Badger friends** comes in…

Comparison

A comparison with the newspaper report might well focus on:

- purpose and audience
- layout and presentational devices
- attitude to the reader and to the subject
- language used
- facts and opinions
- the way the arguments are constructed.

A high-quality answer would analyse the differences, rather than describing them:

The headline in the report is in large, bold, block lettering, and seems to scream at the reader. In comparison, the website uses standard lettering, seems quieter and more friendly. This difference is just as apparent in the language used…

Media texts (1–4)

1 (a) Describe the intended audience and purpose for this advertisement, referring to the content, language and any other features to support your argument. (11)

(b) Suggest the type of publication in which this advertisement might have appeared, and give reasons for your suggestion. (3)

And for those who have everything

Designed to enable you to work from home, The Xerox Document HomeCentre combines the work of a colour inkjet printer, an instant colour photocopier and a colour scanner.

You can slide any document through the front and it will transfer the image to your PC and translate it into text through the software provided. The scanner is also detachable which means you can scan books too.

The WorkCentre, which is the same price, also combines the use of a fax.

Price: £499 (plus VAT)

2 (a) What is the purpose of this cartoon and what audience do you think it is aimed at? (3)

(b) Suggest the type of publication in which it might have appeared, and give reasons for your suggestion. (3)

'What's happened to Deirdre in Coronation Street?'

ANSWERS & TUTORIALS

SCORE

1 (a) The audience for this advertisement will be educated (1) and fairly well-off (1) business people (1) who work from home, (1) are computer-literate (1) and write reports or other documents. (1) The illustration suggests a modern home office, (1) with the computer, large desk and plant (1) all reinforcing the image of a comfortable lifestyle. (1) The headline appeals to snobbery, (1) although in a gently humorous way. (1)

(b) This advertisement probably appeared in a newspaper or magazine read by well-off business people (1) as it assumes they will be interested in the product (1) and would be able to afford the price. (1)

In fact, it was in the *Independent on Sunday* as part of a series which advertises the latest technological gadgets to readers. It is clearly not from a computer magazine, as the language used is not technical, and there is no detailed explanation of how it works or of how effectively it does all the different jobs – in fact, you might have commented that it is being sold more like a fashion accessory than a piece of IT equipment.

2 (a) It is principally to amuse the reader, (1) but also to make the reader feel part of a group with similar interests; (1) it is therefore aimed at those who watch soap operas on television, particularly *Coronation Street*. (1)

(b) It probably comes from a newspaper, or maybe a television listings magazine, with a large readership (1) including many people who watch soap operas. (1)

It is most likely to come from a tabloid newspaper. (1)

That is a perfectly reasonable answer: surprisingly, however, the cartoon was from *The Telegraph*, a broadsheet paper with a largely middle-class readership. It just goes to show how much *Coronation Street* has wheedled its way into the consciousness of the whole nation.

TOTAL

TYPES OF NON-FICTION TEXTS (1)

The main purpose of non-fiction texts is to convey **information or facts**, but this is often presented alongside the author's **ideas or opinions**. Look out for opinions disguised as facts (see page 11) and question the usefulness of arguments (see page 15).

Non-fiction texts include **autobiography**, **biography**, **journals**, **diaries**, **letters**, **essays** and **travel writing**. Because these deal with people's experiences, ideas and attitudes you should read them as though they were literary texts. The **language** used, the people, incidents, places or ideas described, are selected and structured in a **formal** way to have a particular effect on you. Many are written in the first person ('I') so your opinion of the author will influence judgements about the trustworthiness of the text.

In **biography**, the author often writes as though s/he knows all the innermost thoughts and qualities of the subject. You must decide how reliable the author is. In this excerpt, the author has a view of his subject as a businessman which was clearly not shared by everyone:

> Clark was unfairly blamed for the company's troubles, which derived from complacency, failure to modernise and restrictive practices.

You don't know which view is correct, but you must recognise that what is written here is merely an opinion. The opinion is backed by emotive and value-laden words such as 'unfairly', 'blamed', 'complacency', 'failure' and 'restrictive'.

Travel writing often reveals attitudes and prejudices. Paul Theroux in *The Kingdom by the Sea* shows his contempt for seaside holidaymakers, and perhaps some snobbery, when he describes Blackpool as:

> real clutter: the buildings that were not only ugly but also foolish and flimsy, the vacationers sitting under a dark sky with their shirts off, sleeping with their mouths open, emitting hog whimpers.

Words like 'clutter', 'ugly', 'foolish', 'flimsy' and 'hog whimpers' are intended to make you share Theroux's condescending view of these people who visit an unattractive place, sunbathe under 'a dark sky', look foolish and make animal noises. His use of the word 'emitting' puts you on Theroux's side: he knows you are an intelligent person who will understand his language and share his point of view – writers will try to manipulate you in this way.

Journals, diaries and **letters** are usually different. Sometimes they are written for publication (in which case you must read them in the way suggested above). More often they are informal in style and structure, and it is easier to spot the writer's opinions or prejudices. For example, Mary Shelley's diary entry for 6 March 1815 reads:

> Find my baby dead. Send for Hogg. Talk. A miserable day. In the evening read 'Fall of the Jesuits'. Hogg sleeps here.

The plain language, short sentences and jumps from one thought to another underline the spontaneity and real emotion in the writing.

Other non-fiction texts

These include information leaflets and other factual or informative writing, such as encyclopaedia articles or reference books. There is not always an author's name on these, but remember they have been written by someone. Look for evidence of bias in the language or in the selection and presentation of material.

What is in the exam?

For AQA/A, you will possibly get a non-fiction text to compare with another from the media, and you might also be asked about language, argument, fact and opinion or structure. For AQA/B, there will always be an unseen non-fiction text with questions on it, which might well require you to deal with similar features.

Types of non-fiction texts (1–2)

1 Explain three ways in which the style of an autobiography might differ from that of a diary. (3)

2 Read this extract from a travel book.

(a) Explain the author's attitude towards the place and list the words which convey it. (8)

(b) Why has the author chosen to describe these features of the place? (4)

> It was a summer afternoon but so stormy and dark the street lamps were on, and so were the lights in the train. Even the sea was grim here – not rough but motionless and oily, a sort of offshore soup made of sewage and poison.

3 Read the following extract from the review of a new car.

(a) List three pieces of information it gives you. (3)

(b) Explain how the piece also reveals two of the writer's own attitudes. (2)

> Engine noise is intrusive both at rest and at speed. The 0–60 mph sprint takes a soporific 15.8 sec so, as often as not, you drive with the accelerator pressed to the floor. And that, we suspect, is the reason most owners won't come close to Citroen's claimed combined fuel figure of 44.1 mpg.

SCORE

1 The language of an autobiography is likely to be more formal than that of a diary; (1) an autobiography will be more structured (or the material will be more carefully selected) than in a diary; (1) the writer's opinions are likely to be more open or obvious in a diary. (1)

2 **(a)** The writer sees the place as thoroughly unattractive. (1) This is conveyed particularly by the words 'stormy', (1) 'dark', (1) 'grim', (1) 'motionless', (1) 'oily', (1) 'sewage' (1) and 'poison'. (1)

(b) He mentions the contrast between the season and the weather (1) to emphasise how miserable the place is (1) and the appearance of the sea (1) because it is particularly unappealing. (1)

Look for unusual or unexpected words and images when set a question like this. The writer is describing a seaside resort in summer, so the words listed in answer **(a)** are not what you would expect. In answering part **(b)**, you should realise that the aspects of the place the writer chooses to describe are those that you might expect (the weather and the sea), so this reinforces the awfulness of the place.

3 **(a)** Three pieces of information are that engine noise is intrusive, (1) that the car goes from 0–60 in 15.8 seconds (1) and that the combined fuel figure is 44.1 mpg. (1)

(b) The writer's own attitudes are that he does not like engine noise as he calls it 'intrusive' (1) and that he prefers faster cars, as he calls the acceleration of this one 'soporific' (sleepy). (1)

These questions test your ability to identify fact and opinion, which is never as easy as it sounds. For example, is describing the engine noise as 'intrusive' a piece of (factual) information, or merely the writer's opinion? On balance, it probably qualifies as information, since the engine is clearly noisy, although some might find it less annoying than the writer did, which is why his dislike of engine noise generally can be labelled as an opinion (or attitude).

TOTAL

The texts you deal with in the exam are likely to be full of **facts and opinions**. Look at this simple advertisement for car insurance:

Paying £300–£3000 for motor insurance?

We could save you pounds.

Fast, friendly, direct service • Preferential rates • High quality instant cover • Up to 70% No Claims Discount • 24 hour accident recovery • Authorised repair network • Instalment option (Subject to status)

Call 0845 246 0491
or buy on-line
www.privilege.com

privilege*
INSURANCE

Part of The Royal Bank of Scotland Group

Privilege Insurance* 3 Edridge Road, Croydon, Surrey CR9 1AG. Member of the General Insurance Standards Council. Subject to our normal under-writing criteria. Lines open 8am-8pm weekdays and 9am-6pm Sat. Calls may be recorded or monitored. Not available in Northern Ireland.

There are obvious facts: up to 70% No Claims Discount; 24 hour accident recovery; authorised repair network; instalment option; the telephone number; the details on the bottom of the advertisement; and how to contact the company.

There are opinions too: the quality of the service and 'high quality cover'.

Then, there are those details which could be fact or opinion: 'we could save you pounds' and 'preferential rates'.

In the exam, however, you are most likely to be asked **how** facts and opinions are being used, rather than to simply locate them. This means you need to see how they further the **purpose** of the text: how they are used to help the writer develop his or her theme and convince the reader. You will not be expected to find all the facts and opinions and explain them. Rather, you should analyse perhaps three or four usages; or reflect upon how they are used in the text as a whole.

Analysing facts and opinions

When writing about how the facts and opinions are used, you might:

- examine their general effect in the text.
  For example, there could be a long stream of facts followed by an opinion, which makes the reader feel that the opinion is as valid as the facts; or the facts and opinions could be jumbled together, so the reader is unsure which is which, and accepts them all as true;
- look at individual examples.
  For example, 'Fast, friendly, direct service' sounds rapid because of the alliteration ('fast, friendly'), and the ungrammatical phrase seems bustling, cheerful and straight to the point, so the opinion is supposed to sound attractive.

See how facts and opinions are used in this extract from T*he Observer Sport Monthly*:

ANYBODY on the wrong side of the law had better hope they don't bump into Gemma Mitcham. The 20-year-old European karate champion recently qualified as a policewoman and has just started patrolling the streets of Southend.

"I guess you could say anybody that tried anything with me would be a bit unlucky," she says, laughing. "It's only to defend myself, but if I got confronted on the street I'd be pretty confident of being able to handle myself. Being a black belt obviously helps that."

The article opens with an opinion about Gemma, but the second sentence gives a fact about her which would probably lead the reader to believe the opinion, since she is European karate champion. In the second paragraph, we are again given an opinion, supported by a relevant fact ('being a black belt obviously helps . . .').

At times, of course, opinions can be used without immediate facts to back them up. This account by Reginald Thompson of fighting in North Korea relies on the power of vivid, opinionated language for its effect:

Cry Korea

It was a game of blind man's bluff in these wild rugged irregular hills in which the enemy moved freely, easily eluding the groping arms of the Americans by day, and swooping down upon them, blind in the night, with devastating fury and magnificent discipline.

Fact and opinion (1–2)

Read this extract from *Among the Thugs* by Bill Buford.

> The train was a football special, and it had been taken over by supporters. They were from Liverpool, and there were hundreds of them – I had never seen a train with so many people inside – and they were singing in unison: 'Liverpool, la la la, Liverpool, la la la.' The words look silly now, but they did not sound silly. A minute before there had been virtual silence: a misty, sleepy Welsh winter evening. And then this song, pounded out with increasing ferocity, echoing off the walls of the station. A guard had been injured, and as the train stopped, he was rushed off, holding his face. Someone inside was trying to smash a window with a table leg, but the window wouldn't break. A fat man with a red face stumbled out of one of the carriages, and six policemen rushed up to him, wrestled him to the ground and bent his arm violently behind his back. The police were overreacting – the train was so packed that the fat man had popped out of an open door – but the police were frightened...

1 Choose:

- four facts which give essential information and set the scene for when the train arrived (4)
- three facts which show what happened at the station when the train arrived (3)

and explain how the facts have been used by the writer. (3)

2 Write down:

- four opinions about the police (4)
- an explanation of how we are expected to react to these opinions. (2)

3 Explain how facts and opinions are used together in the extract to structure the text and create atmosphere. (4)

SCORE

1 Possible facts to set the scene – any four from:

- the train was a football special
- they were from Liverpool
- there were hundreds of them
- they were singing
- minutes before there had been virtual silence. (4)

Possible facts to show what happened – any three from:

- a guard was rushed off, holding his face
- someone was trying to smash a window with a table leg
- a fat man stumbled out of a carriage
- the police tackled him. (3)

The facts have been used to create a clear picture for the reader (1) and to show a contrast between the station as it was, and how it has become. (1) They also give an impression of noise, violence and disorder. (1)

2 The police seem to be acting in haste ('rushed up to him'), (1) react 'violently', (1) seem to be 'overreacting' (1) but 'were frightened'. (1)

Because of the facts we have already been given, we are supposed to have some sympathy for the police (1) and not criticise them as we might otherwise have done. (1)

3 Any four from:

The writer begins by using facts to set the scene, (1) and to prepare us to accept his opinions about what happened (such as 'pounded out with increasing ferocity'). (1) The fact that they were singing 'Liverpool, la la la' brings the scene to life (1) and we accept his opinion that 'they did not sound silly'. (1) We similarly accept his opinion that 'a sleepy Welsh winter evening' has been spoiled (1) – and the mix of facts and opinions to end the extract gives pictures of how violence has replaced peace. (1) (4 marks in total)

Because facts and opinions and their effects are open to interpretation, different answers would be acceptable. The important point, however, is that the interpretations you present must be relevant, given the purpose of a text; and you must explain and prove your points.

TOTAL

You may be asked a question about how an argument has been constructed or used in a media or non-fiction text. You will be expected to:

- work out exactly what the writer is saying, i.e. what the **purpose** of the text is and what, exactly, the writer's message is;
- be able to explain **how** the argument has been constructed.

Understanding the argument

Understanding the message might mean being much more precise about why the text has been written. For example, the general purpose of an article might be to argue against school uniform, but the exact argument might be:

- that some parents find uniform very expensive;
- that their children resent the fact that they have to wear uniform and refuse to wear any of it outside school;
- that most of the world seems to survive well without school uniforms;
- that it would be a step into the modern world to get rid of uniforms, since they are simply a 'throw-back' to the old days of grammar schools, when a uniform was seen as the sign of a more academic school.

How the argument is constructed

To get good marks, you will probably be expected to identify the linguistic features and general construction the writer has used. This means you need a **critical vocabulary**: a list of those features you might wish to discuss.

For example:

- introduction and conclusion
- development
- examples
- quotations
- figures of speech
- facts and opinions
- humour
- irony
- rhetoric
- contrast
- anecdote
- implication
- exaggeration

and so on.

You are identifying the same features you put into your own writing, and saying **how** they are being used – and to what **effect**.

This letter was sent to a leading women's magazine:

I feel that it is time someone pointed out that not all your readers feel that attracting men is their most important role in life. Almost all your articles seem to dwell on how men will react to a certain fashion or approach, on how to refine our figures or faces so we will be 'beautiful for the summer', or on how to prepare ourselves for deep relationships, by doing everything in our power to please our man. This is all wrong.

Sex is important, but does not have to be everything in our world. Some of us might get as much pleasure from surfing the net – and not just to view those rude websites! We have ranges of interests. As Miriam Dalvi said: "When I go to bed, I want to curl up with a good book, not a new man."

Surely your publication should widen its horizons and stop treating us as stereotypes? Your attitude to women is often limited and limiting and little different from that of men. Perhaps their limitations provide some excuse for treating us as just objects of desire, but you should know better.

Let's have a more varied approach. Let's have a magazine to suit all women. And let's move on into the twenty-first century, not pretend we're still locked into the twentieth.

The argument

This letter says the magazine focuses on how to attract men, but should provide a wider range of articles: women have many interests and are not just the stereotypes men often imagine. The magazine should offer a modern diet of articles for readers.

The construction

The topic sentences in each paragraph stress the main message. Note also these devices:

Paragraph 1: introduction gives examples of what is wrong; powerful, short final sentence

Paragraph 2: humour ('rude websites'); effective quotation

Paragraph 3: rhetoric; sarcastic final sentence

Paragraph 4: conclusion uses repetition to hammer home message; metaphor to conclude.

Following an argument (1–2)

This is the start of an article from *The Observer*.

Older rockers find the beat goes on

By Vanessa Thorpe

The lights go down and the crowd waits. Then slowly, and a little unsteadily, a shadowy figure shuffles to the front of the stage.

Squinting because of his failing eyesight he tries to wriggle his hips, but the replacement operation he had last year allows limited movement.

The crowd goes wild anyway. It sounds like a scene from a sequel to the spoof 'rockumentary' *This Is Spinal Tap*, but this summer, all over Europe and the United States, rock fans of every age will spend between £40 and £150 to watch members of an elite club – the worshipful order of aged rockers.

After two decades devoted to the insipid offerings of manufactured bands, music lovers – many for the first time – are discovering the joys of some of the oldest names in the business.

Seemingly written off as wrinkly has-beens, the likes of AC/DC, Neil Young and The Eagles are back with a vengeance. Backed by slick promotion and marketing gimmicks, venues will rock to Aerosmith, David Gilmour, The Beach Boys, Bill Wyman and 60 year old Bob Dylan.

The appeal of these vintage rockers means the spectacle of middle-aged hellraising is now officially beyond a joke…

1 How does the writer interest the reader in the first paragraph? (5)

2 Explain how humour is used to develop the argument. (5)

3 In the third paragraph, what are we supposed to think of modern performers? (3)

4 Why is the final sentence in the extract effective? (3)

5 How would you expect the article to continue, and why? (4)

ANSWERS & TUTORIALS

SCORE

1 The introduction uses an anecdote (1) and begins with a short, dramatic sentence. (1) There is excitement and expectation ('the crowd waits'). (1) There is mystery ('a shadowy figure'), (1) but also comedy ('unsteadily' and 'shuffles'). (1)

2 To keep the reader's attention, the writer develops the ridiculous image of an aged performer ('Squinting… he tries to wriggle his hips'), (1) exaggerating his disabilities ('the replacement operation'). (1) She also expects us to laugh at the audience enjoying the spectacle, (1) and mocks old rockers by using irony so they are like a religious movement ('the worshipful order'). (1) Presumably, we should see this return of old stars as laughable. (1)

3 More modern artists are contrasted with has-beens, (1) but their music sounds less impressive ('insipid offerings'), less real ('manufactured bands'). (1) It is implied they do not bring 'the joys' of the oldies. (1)

Through these paragraphs, the writer concentrates on purpose and audience: presenting the story, beginning to reveal why the old stars are still popular and making the article lighthearted, to appeal to broadsheet readers.

4 Metaphorically, the artists seem like appealing rich wine ('vintage'); (1) then there is what seems an oxymoron (contradictory phrase) – 'middle-aged hellraising'; (1) but at the end the paragraph seems more serious. (1)

5 The last sentence in the extract implies the article will move on to more serious matters. (1) It might explain why old rockers are still needed; (1) and perhaps what they earn, since money has already been mentioned. (1) Although the writer has been poking fun at the performers, we feel she will be discussing their likely successes, because they have been backed by 'slick promotion and marketing gimmicks'. (1)

You might have produced a different answer to the final question, but that does not matter as long as you have noted progression in the argument, and have justified your opinions by referring directly to the text.

TOTAL

Structure in non-fiction/media texts (1)

Structural devices

Most non-fiction and media texts are put together carefully so as to have maximum impact on their intended audiences. This is true even of 'private' texts such as diaries or letters, which will usually be structured in narrative or chronological ways to capture the writer's idea or point of view. More 'public' texts – such as information leaflets or magazine articles – will usually show a wide range of features. This is because there are often business-related reasons for their need to succeed.

Most of these additional features are intended to ensure that the reader understands the message or **purpose** of the text in two main ways. Firstly, by presenting information in a logical way and/or in a way which will capture your interest and imagination. Secondly, by presenting text in small units so that you are able to take it in easily and think about it as you go. You are less likely to become bored by it, and more likely to stick with it to the end. Breaking text up in this way also allows it to be presented attractively (as you will see in more detail on pages 23–24).

Look at this advertisement for homes in the USA:

Florida

Largest selection of 3, 4 and 5 bedroom houses in Orlando, New Port Richey, South West Gulf Coast

- ★ 3 bedroom pool homes from $125,000
- ★ 4 bedroom pool homes from $145,000
- ★ Golf course developments
- ★ 80% mortgages available
- ★ Full management and rental services

For information pack:

Tel: 01432 992655 **Fax: 01432 793353**

F.J. Cook & Sons

Structure in non-fiction/media texts (2)

This example shows use of the following structural features:

- A **clear heading** to attract the attention of targeted readers.
- Although there is only a small amount of text, it is full of **relevant information**.
- Key details are in a **bullet-pointed list** to avoid information overload.
- Different aspects of the information (e.g. contacts for further details) are **separated** to help readers easily find what they need to know.

These are some of the most common structural devices found in printed non-fiction/media texts – whatever their length, purpose or audience.

Other devices

Other devices to look out for include the use of graphical information (particularly charts or tables) to convey numerical or financial information, or maps, diagrams and timetables to convey travel information.

The purpose of such structural devices is to ensure that the reader quickly gains whatever information the writer wishes to convey. When responding to non-fiction/media texts you should always write about structural features with these questions in mind:

- Does the structuring of the content help the writer achieve the desired purpose?
- If so, how? If not, what are the shortcomings of the structure?
- What effect is this text likely to have on its target audience?

The last point is important. If a piece of text is aimed, say, at teenagers then it is not reasonable to criticise it on the grounds that older people would not understand the use of slang or colloquial language. Similarly, do not criticise an advertisement for pensions aimed at older people because it is 'boring' to a teenage reader.

Structure in non-fiction/media texts (1–2)

1 (a) Identify five structural features used in this advertisement for a house to let. (5)

(b) Comment on how these features might help it achieve the desired effect on its target audience. (5)

Howard Prince Stepney & Partners

THE INTERNATIONAL LETTING AGENCY

Windsor • Cheam • Richmond

TO LET

Superb contemporary four bedroom house on the banks of the River Thames within walking distance of Richmond

£5,500 pcm

Telephone: 020 8498 3144

2 (a) Identify five structural features in this information from *What Car?* magazine. (5)

(b) Comment on their effectiveness. (5)

Car supermarket shopping – and main dealer prices

Car supermarket	Make/model	Year	Market price	Dealer price	Saved
Sanderson Motorhouse, Cheltenham	Ford Mondeo 1.8 LX 5dr	97R	£10,995	£11,495	**£500**
	Vauxhall Vectra 1.8 LS 5dr	97R	£10,995	£11,295	**£300**
Car Supermarket, Newport **Best Deal**	Ford Mondeo 1.8 LX 5dr	97R	£10,799	£11,495	**£696**
	Vauxhall Vectra 1.8 LS 5dr	97R	£10,595	£11,295	**£700**
Lex Autosales, Bristol	Ford Mondeo 1.8 LX TD	96P	£8999	£9945	**£946**
	Peugeot 406 1.9 L TD	96P	£9489	£10,195	**£706**
Discount Cars Direct, Sunningdale	Ford Mondeo 2.0 GLX 5dr	97P	£10,299	£11,495	**£1196**
	Vauxhall Vectra 1.8 LS 5dr	97P	£9999	£10,795	**£796**
Carland, Thurrock	Ford Mondeo 1.8 LX 5dr	97P	£10,800	£11,095	**£295**
	Vauxhall Vectra 1.8 GLS 5dr	97P	£10,500	£10,995	**£495**

ANSWERS & TUTORIALS

SCORE

1 (a) Structural features:

- main heading (1)
- bullet pointing (1)
- brief text (1)
- use of abbreviation (1)
- telephone number separate (1)

(b) The main heading makes the purpose/audience of the advertisement clear. (1) Bullet-pointing the locations of the firm makes it easy for readers to see if there is a branch convenient for them. (1) The text about the house is brief but it contains sufficient information for readers to decide if it interests them. (1) An abbreviation ('pcm': per calendar month) is used which saves space and would be understood by the target audience. (1) The telephone number of the firm is separate and in **bold** to encourage readers to follow up the advertisement. (1)

Notice how all the comments are related to the **audience** and **purpose** of the advertisement. When you are reading any non-fiction/media text, make sure that one of the first decisions you make is to identify the purpose and target audience. This will make it easier for you to comment on the effectiveness of the techniques used.

2 (a) Structural features:

- clear main heading (1)
- use of table (1)
- column headings (1)
- brief text (1)
- use of a flash (1)

(b) The clear main heading sets out the purpose of the information. (1)

The use of a table enables an easy comparison of the information in the text. (1)

Column headings further clarify the information. (1)

The text itself is very brief and so guides the reader to the most significant information. (1)

The use of the 'Best Deal' flash quickly draws the reader's attention to the highlight of the information. (1)

TOTAL

PRESENTATIONAL DEVICES (1)

These are more to do with how the text is **presented**. There is some overlap here with structural devices (see pages 19–20). For example, bullet points or headlines are really both structural and presentational. All the devices discussed on page 20, and those detailed here, are concerned with **achieving desired effects** on particular audiences. You should therefore respond to the use of presentational devices in the same way as to structural devices. You should ask yourself these questions:

- Do the devices help the writer to achieve the desired purpose?
- If so, how? If not, why have the devices not worked?
- What effect is this text likely to have on its target audience?

Frames

These may be placed around parts of a text, or around the whole text. The effect in either case should be to draw the reader's eye to something significant. Look out for which parts of a text are highlighted in this way and which are not. Sometimes the absence of frames can be used to divert attention from details which the writer does not want to stand out – such as details of additional charges or product guarantees.

Illustrations

These may serve a number of purposes. Above all, they can make dull text look more attractive and therefore more interesting. At the same time, they may present an image of the information, product or idea which the writer is trying to promote. Consider how realistic or honest illustrations are – sometimes new cars or houses will be represented by an 'artist's impression'. Ask yourself 'why?' Is it because the actual product doesn't exist? Or can the 'impression' impress more than the real thing?

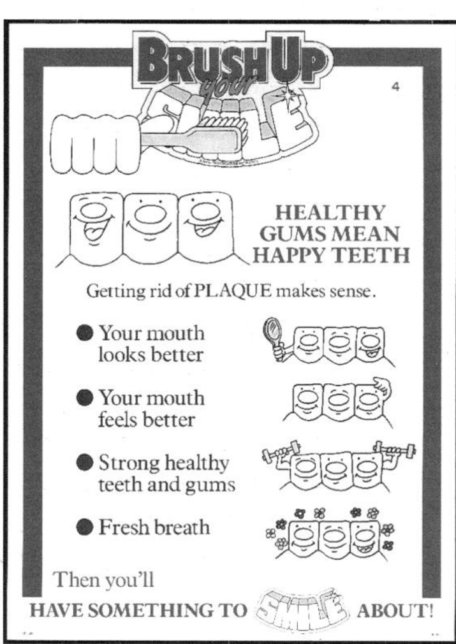

Colour

Colour is often used sparingly (as in this book) as it is expensive to reproduce. Although colour can make text eye-catching (see poster on page 23), over-fussy or poor use of colours can be distracting. They can make text more difficult to read, rather than more attractive.

Fonts

The style and size of **different fonts** may affect the way a reader reacts to text. For example, some fonts have a more 'serious' or formal appearance, while others are more obviously informal. Some styles are associated closely with particular eras (e.g. the 1970s or 1980s) or even individual products. Some styles may be associated with feelings or atmospheres. For example, a ruined castle, or a horror film, might use a 'gothic' or 'medieval' font in their promotional literature. Larger fonts may be used to emphasise particular aspects of a text. The so-called 'small print' may hide less attractive information. Text may be in **bold**, in *italics* or underlined in various ways, to add to the impact of different font styles and sizes.

Ghost Train

Logos and symbols

Logos are used mostly to fix the image of a company or organisation in the reader's mind so that it is instantly recognised when met again. Some advertising relies on well-known logos and does not mention the company name at all. The effect of this can be to make the reader feel as though s/he belongs almost to an exclusive 'club' of those who understand the logo, and can therefore make them more responsive to the advertisement. Symbols such as ticks, crosses, pairs of scissors and so on can be space-savers, and thus cost-savers. They can also be helpful to readers.

Presentational devices (1–2)

1 (a) In this advertisement for home insurance, identify five presentational and/or structural features. (5)

(b) Comment on how each feature contributes to the success of the advertisement. (5)

Discount type	% discount
Approved alarm fitted †	5%
Approved security locks fitted* †	5%
Any applicant aged 50 or over	5%
Joint buildings and contents policy	10%
An excess is the first part of any claim you have to pay. You may choose to change the standard £50 excess to one of the following:	
£25	£5 annual charge
£100	5% discount
£200	12.5% discount
Please note the excess for personal belongings and pedal cycles is £25 and this cannot be charged. * The discount does not apply in areas where we require certain extra security measures. † Ask for a copy of our Minimum Standard of Security leaflet to check if you qualify for our alarm and security locks discounts.	

2 (a) Identify five presentational features used in this advertisement. (5)

(b) Comment on how effectively they attract the attention of an appropriate target audience. (5)

THE COPPER KETTLE COFFEE SHOP
WHITE ROCK FALLS

Visit the newly refurbished **Visitors Centre**
(with educational 'hands-on' exhibition).*
Relax over coffee or a light lunch in our new Coffee Shop
where emphasis is on value for money
and a warm welcome awaits visitors and locals alike.

Opening times:

End of Oct. – 1 April Mon – Fri 10am – 4pm
1 April – end of Oct. 7 days a week 10am – 5pm

For more information or a sample menu ring: 01699 336426

*Child friendly and with access for the disabled

1 (a) Presentational/structural features:
- table format (1)
- reversed colours of the column headings (1)
- font used (1)
- words simple and straightforward (1)
- footnotes (1)

(b) A table format is used to clarify what could be complicated information. (1)
The reversed colours of the column headings make them stand out as titles. (1)
The font used is simple and 'clean' for ease of reading/so as not to distract the reader's attention from the potentially complicated text. (1)
The words in the text are straightforward to keep the message as simple as possible. (1)
Footnotes are used to clarify and extend the information where necessary or to keep unnecessary extra words out of the main table. (1)
This is an example of text which is unlikely to be exciting, given its subject matter and the need to convey detailed information. However, the controlled use of appropriate structures and presentational devices can make the text effective and efficient.

2 (a) Presentational features:
- decorative frame (1)
- upper case headlines (1)
- teacup logo (1)
- some use of text in bold (1)
- short paragraphs (1)

(b) The decorative frame makes the advertisement stand out. (1)
The upper case headlines make the location of the coffee shop clear. (1)
The teacup logo shows the nature of the advertisement at a glance and attracts the target audience immediately. (1)
Some use of **bold** type emphasises important details. (1)
Short paragraphs break up the text for easy reading. (1)

TOTAL

USE OF LANGUAGE (1)

All texts are written for a purpose. Skilful writers will manipulate (i.e. control) your response to a text through the range of techniques they use. You have already looked at some of these techniques, but the most valuable weapon a writer has is **individual words**. Look at this fairly typical advertisement for a new house:

Large detached house with
four double bedrooms,
all with bathrooms.
Set in a charming village environment.
Convenient access to M4.
Home exchange available.

£349,950

Similar housetypes to be built

Honeypot Grove, Holywell, Berkshire
Follow signs towards Holywell from junction 8/9 off the M4.
Sales office and superb showhome open from 10am to 6pm, Thursday to Tuesday (Monday 2pm to 6pm)
Tel: 01826 7006213

Individual words such as 'large', 'detached', 'charming', 'convenient' and 'superb' are all examples of opinions disguised as facts. There are also whole phrases designed to influence the reader's feelings:

- 'charming village environment' is intended to evoke a warm glow of belonging to a community with old-fashioned values;
- 'convenient access to M4' shows that the house isn't too far away from the city;
- 'home exchange available' reassures the prospective buyer that they won't need to sell their existing house.

However, note the words in very small print beneath the illustration – 'Similar housetypes to be built'. This is not avoiding the truth, but it does point to the fact that the picture is not actually the house for sale.

Use of language (2)

The language of non-fiction, particularly that of advertisements, often appeals to our emotions, such as snobbery. The house advertisement on page 27 does that. Although the language is restrained (i.e. not 'over the top'), it nevertheless suggests that this is a house for a successful businessperson.

Other types of non-fiction texts, such as autobiography or travel writing, often use language in a more literary way. This is intended to engage the reader's imagination. As an example, Roald Dahl mentions in *Going Solo*:

> **sinister vultures waiting like feathered undertakers for death to come along and give them something to work on.**

Humour is often used in texts like these. It may be kindly or, more often than not, pointed and condemning. Read this extract from *Notes From a Small Island* by Bill Bryson:

> **Bradford's role in life is to make every place else in the world look better in comparison, and it does this very well.**

When commenting on humour remember to explain the effect it has on the reader. Is it to make a sort of bond between the writer and reader? Or is it to make sharp criticism of someone or something? Or is it just to show off the author's verbal dexterity (clever use of words)?

Verbal dexterity is often used by writers of media texts which advertise products. '**Catchphrases**' which become associated with chocolate bars or soft drinks are important to the success of one kind of non-fiction writer. The idea is to fix certain products in our minds by coming up with memorable phrases. These 'catchphrases' rely on devices such as rhyme and repetition ('A Mars a day helps you work, rest and play') or literary language that is slightly ridiculous (such as describing an Australian lager as the 'amber nectar'). Alliteration, puns, onomatopoeia and (often far-fetched) imagery are all used by writers when advertising products. (Look back at pages 19–20 to remind yourself of these devices and the effects they can achieve.)

Use of language (1–2)

1 Look at this restaurant advertisement.

(a) Pick out four examples of language designed to have a particular effect on the reader. (4)

(b) Comment on how this language does appeal to the reader. (4)

SHAWS RESTAURANT HAWES

Fine continental cuisine served in charming surroundings. The menu offers plenty of interesting and intriguing combinations professionally prepared for you by our chef **Anton Deschamps.**

Open Tuesday to Sunday – evening and lunches

Please book for weekend meals to avoid disappointment.

To book your table tel 01699 745866

2 In this extract from *And when did you last see your father?* the author, Blake Morrison, evokes various feelings through his use of language.

(a) Identify and comment on three examples which make the underground train seem threatening. (6)

(b) Identify and comment on three examples which describe the people around him. (6)

...then I hear the inevitable growling and swelling in the tunnel, the sleek rat springing hyperactive and lethal from its trap. The carriage is full of men, every one a killer, brow-lines of rage and torment sculpted as if with hammer and chisel. Next to me is a close-cropped twenty-year-old in a leather jacket, with an AIDS INTERNATIONAL DAY sticker. He crouches by the pneumatic doors next to his dog, a beautiful grey velvety Weimaraner. The dog is nervous to be travelling in this thing, the rattling steel, the shaky floor. Every so often it gives a little howl, and when it does its leathered owner yanks on its collar and pulls its face up hard against his, staring it out, boss, disciplinarian, torturer.

SCORE

1 (a) Language:
- 'fine continental cuisine' (1)
- 'charming surroundings' (1)
- 'interesting and intriguing combinations' (1)
- 'professionally prepared' (1)

(b) Comments:
- 'Fine continental cuisine' appeals to readers who believe they have a taste for sophisticated food. (1)
- 'Charming surroundings' appeals to readers' appreciation of an appealing environment. (1)
- 'Interesting and intriguing combinations' appeals to readers who feel they are adventurous in their eating habits. (1)
- 'Professionally prepared' appeals to readers who believe they are entitled to the best. (1)

This advertisement is geared at appealing to a gentle kind of snobbery among its readers. Providing the name of the chef is another example of this, which you might have picked out. Also the suggestion that you might need to book at weekends to avoid disappointment.

2 (a) The train:
- 'growling and swelling' (1) gives the train the sound of a fierce creature (1)
- '...the sleek rat...trap' (1) continues the idea of an attacking creature (1)
- 'the rattling steel, the shaky floor' (1) makes the train seem insecure, unsafe, even dangerous. (1)

(b) The people:
- 'every one a killer...hammer and chisel' (1) makes the men sound violent and aggressive (1)
- 'leathered owner' (1) makes the man sound tough and uncaring (1)
- 'boss, disciplinarian, torturer' (1) reinforces the previous images by making this man sound uncaring, cruel and selfish (1)

TOTAL

COMPARING TEXTS (1)

One of the skills which you can expect to be examined on is your ability to **compare** texts (this will be in Section A of Paper 1 for AQA examinations). You might be asked to compare in terms of:

- purpose and audience
- language
- use of facts and opinions
- argument and structure
- presentational devices and layout
- success.

For AQA Specification A, it is likely you will be given a main or 'stem' question like:

> Which of the texts is most successful?

and will then be told what to look at in detail:

> Compare the texts by writing about:
> • purpose and audience • language • presentational devices.

If you are following AQA Specification B, it is possible you could be given a stem question, then a series of questions on the two texts, just one of which involves comparison.

Whichever approach is used, the important element in your answer is your ability to deal with both texts and make valid comparisons. You will need to use appropriate vocabulary, like 'similarly', 'on the other hand', 'in contrast', 'but in the second text…' and so on. Simply making a point about each text, without linking them, will lose you marks. Always ensure you make the comparison clear – and make sure that, as you compare them, you are still dealing with the stem question.

Spot the differences here:

The first text is written for old people and is a newspaper article. The second text is an advertisement that might be found in a sports magazine.

The first text appeals to its target audience, old people, through the way language is used. For example, it says... In contrast, the second text is an advertisement which tries hard to interest young people but is likely to fail, because...

Two views of teachers:

When the teacher knew best

People talk of school bullies and playground gangs, reminisce about exam nerves, or bad school food, or detention, or the cane, or the simple terrors of sports day.

But the most frightening thing I encountered during my school days was a big Scots maths teacher with a taste for violence.

His weapon of choice may only have been a wooden-handled board duster, but his acid wit, a voice whose nearest equivalent was fingernails being scraped down a blackboard, and the sheer presence of this six-foot-something man with a shock of wiry white hair and a huge academic black cloak, made McLeod a man to be feared...

The Yorkshire Evening Post, Simon Jenkins

Escape for head who allowed cheating

A primary head who admitted that he allowed 11-year-old pupils to cheat in national tests, has been told he can continue teaching.

The General Teaching Council for England heard that David Hopkins, headteacher at Whitenights school, Reading, had let pupils change answers to maths papers hours after they had taken the test. He also allowed pupils who had taken science papers to mix with those who had not.

Mr Hopkins claimed that he was under pressure to improve the school s position in the league tables

TES, Becky Sharpe

If you were asked how teachers are presented in the texts, and to compare the language and structure of the two texts, your answer should be along these lines:

The first text gives a frightening picture of the teacher, using words like "frightening" and "violence", whereas the second text uses words like "let" and "allowed", and the headteacher seems much more...

Whilst the first text begins with a list of school horrors, then links them with the terrifying Mr McLeod, so that it is still unclear exactly what the columnist's point will be, the second text opens with a summary of what has happened to David Hopkins, before giving the facts of the case, therefore presenting a more sympathetic picture...

Comparing texts (1–2)

Compare these two texts, by writing about:

1 purpose and audience (4)
2 presentational devices (4)
3 language (6)
4 facts and opinions. (6)

Ugly

That's the only word for the way some people treat animals. Like Holly, who was shoved down a drain in a plastic bin liner. She nearly died before we were able to rescue her, and sadly lost an eye.

Every day we protect cats and dogs from cruelty and ignorance. To help, please phone this number now and make a small regular donation of £3 a month. Without you we just couldn't survive.

REG. CHARITY 219099

0870 3335 999

We receive no government funding

BBC HOMEPAGE | WORLD SERVICE | EDUCATION

BBC NEWS

You are in: UK
Monday, 23 July, 2001, 11:25 GMT 12:25 UK

Microwaved cat woman avoids jail

Front Page
World
UK
England
Northern Ireland
Scotland
Wales
UK Politics
Business
Sci/Tech
Health
Education
Entertainment
Talking Point
In Depth
AudioVideo

A woman who cooked the family cat in a microwave oven after one of the animal's fleas bit her on the leg has escaped jail.

Nadine Trewin, 31, was banned from keeping animals for five years and was sentenced to a two-year community rehabilitation order.

But the RSPCA, which brought the case to court, has condemned the ban as "far too lenient".

RSPCA spokeswoman Claire Kennet said: "We feel she should have received a lifetime ban because the act was deliberate."

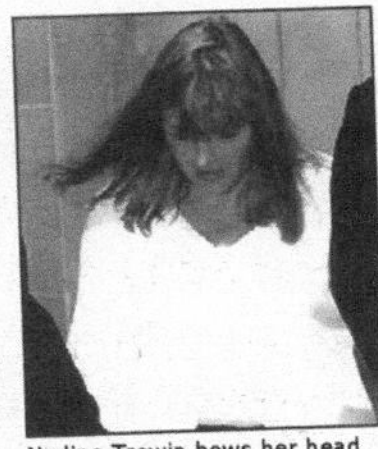

Nadine Trewin bows her head outside court

Trewin, a mother-of-two, had changed her plea and admitted cruelty during a trial at Horsham magistrates' court last month.

The court heard that on 23 March, 2000, Trewin, who had drunk seven cans of lager and almost two bottles of wine, became angry with the cat when she was bitten by the flea.

Advanced search options

Launch console for latest audio/video

BBC RADIO NEWS
BBC ONE TV NEWS
WORLD NEWS SUMMARY
BBC NEWS 24 BULLETIN
PROGRAMMES GUIDE

See also:

20 Jun 01 | UK
Woman 'cooked cat in microwave'

Internet links:

The Court Service
RSPCA

The BBC is not responsible for the content of external internet sites

Top UK stories now:

Postcode lottery in GP services
Leanne killer jailed for life
Tories attack Brixton drugs scheme
Straw defends arms sales change
IVF mix-up heads for court
Police shoot man on the M6
New challenge excites Venables
Judge urges life sentence shake-up

Links to more UK stories are at the foot of the page.

ANSWERS & TUTORIALS

SCORE

1 The advertisement is aiming to raise funds for the RSPCA, (1) targeting adults who are willing to offer 'a small regular donation'. (1) In contrast, the web page gives details of a news story. (1) Its audience is likely to be internet users who are following the news or researching projects. (1)

2 The advertisement uses white writing carved out of black to emphasise the word 'ugly' and grab attention. (1) The puppy produces an emotive response, touching our sympathies. (1) (Possible additional points on the telephone number and RSPCA logo.) The web page, on the other hand, focuses us on the images of justice in the top photograph, (1) and shows the convicted woman bowing her head (with guilt?), so she is named, shown and shamed. (1)

3 The advertisement begins with two ungrammatical sentences, seeming conversational. (1) Vocabulary is used similarly: 'shoved' (1). Throughout, the language is emotive: 'nearly died', 'without you we couldn't survive'. (1) The web page, though, deals with its story with no apparent emotion. The report opens with facts (1) expecting readers to be literate, using relatively difficult vocabulary ('community rehabilitation order'). (1) Paragraphs are kept short, helping readers take in information more easily. (1)

4 The facts in the advertisement involve the dog's injuries and details of the charity. (1) We are expected to respond positively to them because of how the opinions of the RSPCA are presented, to touch our affections ('sadly'; 'she nearly died'). (2) The facts on the web page describe what Nadine Trewin did (1) and since they are so horrible, we tend to accept the opinions of the RSPCA spokeswoman: 'she should have received a lifetime ban'. (2)

More points could have been made in these answers. You can be confident that the examiners will accept them if they are valid and proven.

TOTAL

Sound effects

When you read a poem, what does it sound like? Do the sounds have anything to do with its subject matter? If you speak a poem out loud, how much effort does it take to pronounce the words? Do the sounds of the words, and the effort it takes to make them, help you share the poet's feelings or sense the atmosphere the poet is trying to create?

When Wilfred Owen, a soldier-poet of the First World War, writes about '*the merciless iced east winds that knive us*', the sounds (that is, all the *c*s, *s*s and *i*s) make you feel as though you are experiencing the biting cold, and sharing his despair.

Owen's line shows examples of both **alliteration** (when the same sound is repeated, for example the *c*s, *s*s and *i*s) and of **onomatopoeia** (when the sound of a word imitates the sound of what it describes). 'Wind' is an onomatopoeic word, as you make a blowing sound when you pronounce it. So is 'knive', as the sound of the word is sharp and violent, just like the effect of the cold wind it describes.

Poets often use alliteration and onomatopoeia together. Their choice of words may also be influenced by the physical effort the reader needs to make when speaking them out loud. In the Owen extract, 'knive' ends with a rasping *v* sound, and the *c*s and *s*s in the other words are very forceful too as you need to force air between your teeth to pronounce them.

In complete contrast, Lord Alfred Tennyson uses gentle, soothing sounds in the following lines from his poem *In Memoriam*. These require little effort on the speaker's part and so reinforce the alliteration and onomatopoeia. They create the effect of a hot, drowsy summer afternoon.

The moan of doves in immemorial elms
And the murmuring of innumerable bees

Imagery

Poets often use original **imagery** to convey their meaning. The image may relate an object, place or emotion to something with which you are familiar, so that you can share the poet's feelings. When Gillian Clarke writes '*Like peaty water sun slowly fills the long brown room*' she is using a **simile**, where the word 'like' makes a direct comparison of one thing (sunlight) to something else (peaty water). In this example, the simile helps you picture a room which remains rather gloomy and mysterious despite the brightness which comes into it. It allows you to share the feelings of apprehension which the poem describes.

Imagery may be used to shock you into seeing something in a different way, if the poet compares the familiar or comfortable with something frightening or disturbing. For example, to Ted Hughes 'thistles'

> **are like pale hair and the gutturals of dialects.**
> **Every one manages a plume of blood.**

Here there is a simile in the first sentence. The reference to 'a plume of blood' is a **metaphor** – there isn't really blood on the thistles, just a purply-red colouring on their tips, but the image suggests the violence Ted Hughes associates with thistles.

Hughes also uses the technique known as **personification**, when objects or places are made to seem alive by the words used to describe them. In the final lines of Hughes' poem, personification is combined with metaphor and simile to reinforce the threat he sees in thistles:

> **Then they grow grey like men.**
> **Mown down, it is a feud. Their sons appear,**
> **Stiff with weapons, fighting back over the**
> **same ground.**

Reading poetry (1–2)

1 **(a)** Identify the examples of alliteration in these lines from Carol Ann Duffy's *Valentine*. (2)

(b) What effect do they have? (2)

> **I am trying to be truthful.**
> **Not a cute card or kissogram.**
> **I give you an onion.**

2 **(a)** How is onomatopoeia used in the following lines by Gillian Clarke, (3) and **(b)** what effect does it have on the reader? (2)

> **War planes have been at it all day long**
> **shaking the world, strung air**
> **humming like pianos when children bang the keys.**

3 Explain simile, metaphor and personification. (3)

4 The following lines are from a poem by Seamus Heaney in which he describes the death of his four-year-old brother.

(a) Identify a simile and a metaphor. (2)

(b) Explain the meaning of each. (2)

(c) What effect do they have on the reader? (2)

> **Wearing a poppy bruise on his left temple,**
> **He lay in the four-foot box as in his cot.**

5 **(a)** How is personification used in this extract from a war poem by Wilfred Owen, (1) and **(b)** to what effect? (1)

> **Dawn massing in the east her melancholy army**
> **Attacks once more in ranks on shivering ranks of gray.**

ANSWERS & TUTORIALS

SCORE

1 **(a)** 'trying to be truthful' (1) and 'cute card or kissogram' (1)
(b) The 't' sounds are sharp, as if the poet is attempting to make her statement clear and definite. (1)
The 'k' sounds are giggly; or trying to sound childish or insincere. (1)

2 **(a)** The onomatopoeic words are 'shaking', (1) 'humming' (1) and 'bang'. (1)
(b) 'Shaking' and 'bang' relate to the mention of war planes and reinforce the sense of violence and/or fear, (1) while 'humming' creates a feeling of tension. (1)

You need to hear a poem inside your mind to judge the impact of sound effects. Think also about the physical effort needed to produce certain sounds or to pronounce words.

3 A simile compares one thing with something else, using words such as 'like' or 'as'. (1) A metaphor describes something directly as though it were something else. (1) Personification is making an inanimate object seem human, or alive. (1)

4 **(a)** 'A poppy bruise' is a metaphor; (1) 'As in his cot' is a simile. (1)
(b) The metaphor conveys the colour, shape and size of the bruise; (1) the simile suggests sleep and/or peacefulness. (1)
(c) The metaphor saddens the reader by reinforcing the theme of death through the association of the poppy with Remembrance Day; (1) the simile emphasises the fact that the body is that of a young child and makes the reader feel a sense of waste. (1)

Notice how an image may require you to look beyond the immediate text to gain the author's full meaning, as in this metaphor which refers to a tradition of remembrance.

5 **(a)** The break of day is compared to an enemy attack. (1)
(b) This makes it seem that even the forces of nature have a personal grudge against the soldiers. (1)

TOTAL

Purpose, tone and attitude

When you respond to a poem, you need to think – what is it about and why was it written? Does it make you see situations in a new light or understand feelings in greater depth? When Gillian Clarke describes her car, left near a building which was being demolished, in her poem *Jac Codi Baw* as

> splattered with the stone's blood, smoky with ghosts.

her **purpose** is to help us reflect on how much is actually being destroyed.

Tone refers to the way in which the poet addresses you. It may be to question you or challenge your thinking, as when George Herbert writes in *Jordan*:

> Who says that fictions only and false hair
> Become a verse?

Or the tone may be quite matter-of-fact. Nissim Ezekiel begins the poem *Night of the Scorpion*:

> I remember the night my mother
> was stung by a scorpion.

Attitude means the poet's viewpoint: is the 'I' in the poem the poet him or herself, or is the writing ironically putting forward ideas the poet does not hold? In the lines by Gillian Clarke above, it seems quite clear that she is expressing her own attitude of sadness. But to decide if Simon Armitage is being honest in his poem which begins

> I am very bothered when I think
> of the bad things I have done in my life.

you would need to consider the whole poem very carefully.

Form

The **form** of a poem can also affect your response to it. Regular rhyme and rhythm may often create a happy, light-hearted mood and convey simple ideas – or the poet may use the form ironically to contrast with, and emphasise, a sombre message. This is what William Blake does in his poem *London*:

> **But most thro' midnight streets I hear**
> **How the youthful harlot's curse**
> **Blasts the new-born infant's tear,**
> **And blights with plagues the marriage hearse.**

Poems which have an irregular rhythm and little, or no, rhyme can seem more like a conversation. It may feel as though the poet is talking directly to you, especially if the language is blunt and everyday rather than formal. This is Seamus Heaney in his poem *The Early Purges*:

> **I was six when I first saw kittens drown.**
> **Dan Taggart pitched them, 'the scraggy wee shits',**
> **Into a bucket**

Sometimes the form of a poem can imitate its meaning, as in the opening of this poem by Alice Walker, *Poem at Thirty-Nine*, where the shortening lines seem to illustrate her tired father running out of energy:

> **How I miss my father.**
> **I wish he had not been**
> **so tired**
> **when I was**
> **born.**

Always try to comment on the form of a poem: it is chosen for a purpose by the poet, as carefully as the ideas, words and images are chosen.

Reading poetry (3–4)

1 How would you define purpose, tone and attitude in a poem? (3)

2 **(a)** What do you think was William Blake's purpose in writing the following poem? (3)

(b) What is the tone of the poem, and what attitudes does it display? (3)

O Rose, thou art sick!
The invisible worm,
That flies in the night,
In the howling storm,
Has found out thy bed
Of crimson joy,
And his dark secret love
Does thy life destroy.

3 What could you write about if you were asked to discuss the form of a poem? (5)

4 **(a)** What are the features of the form in which these lines (by Maya Angelou) are written? (4)

(b) How effectively does the form suit the poet's purpose? (2)

I go boo
Make them shoo
I make fun
Way them run
I won't cry
So they fly
I just smile
They go wild
Life doesn't frighten me at all.

SCORE

1 Purpose is why the poem has been written – what the poet wants you to think about. (1) Tone is the way in which the poet addresses you. (1) Attitude is the point of view expressed. (1)

2 **(a)** Blake's purpose is to remind readers that even beautiful objects like a rose do not last for ever (1) and can be spoilt or destroyed by unseen enemies; (1) in other words, you need to be on the look out for trouble or danger all the time. (1)

(b) The tone is direct (1) and challenging; (1) Blake's attitude is one of concern. (1)

The purpose of a poem may be 'between the lines', as in this case – it is not really about a rose at all. When answering a question like this, look at the language and imagery used to help you suggest meanings. There are no right or wrong answers, but some will be more sensible than others. So pay close attention to tone when describing attitude and purpose.

3 You could describe the patterns of rhythm (1) and rhyme (1) in the poem, and whether the language is formal or informal. (1) You could also describe any particular verse patterns. (1) You should remember to comment on the effects all these features have on you. (1)

Whenever you are responding to poetry you must pay constant attention to the **language** of the poem. This may be done when you are considering sound effects and imagery, as well as when you are looking at the structure of the poem or at its tone, attitudes and purpose – all of these aspects are affected by the poet's choice of words.

4 **(a)** The extract is made up of four pairs of rhyming lines (1) and a longer line at the end which does not rhyme. (1) The language is colloquial or everyday. (1) The rhythm is simple and regular until the last line. (1)

(b) The effect is of a cheerful and/or confident poet, (1) and the changed rhythm of the last line emphasises it as the message of the poem. (1)

TOTAL

Poems from different cultures and traditions (1)

Depending on which specification you are taking, you may have to study a number of poems from cultures around the world, then write about two poems in the exam.

If you are taking **AQA Specification A**, the poems are in your Anthology. There are two poetry clusters, each containing eight poems. In the exam, there will be two questions on poems from different cultures, and you will have to answer one of them. If you are studying both clusters, you should be able to answer either question. If, however, you are only studying one cluster, you will have to answer the question set on those particular poems. It will involve comparing two of the poems.

If you are taking **AQA Specification B**, the pre-release poems arrive in January prior to the exam. There will be between eight and ten poems. On the exam paper, there will be a previously unseen poem, which you will have to compare with one of the poems you have studied. There are likely to be a number of short questions, or a stem question which has bullet points to which you must respond.

The poems need to be analysed in the same way that you would analyse any poem. You will need to be able to write about:

- the message and themes in the poems
- the way the poems are structured
- how language is used by the poets.

You will also be expected, in any answer, to write about the different cultures highlighted in the poems: in other words, what makes them **culturally distinctive**. This might mean writing about families, or living conditions, or politics or emotional ties, or whatever the poems are about. This will be straightforward, though, because the questions will be set so that you cannot avoid writing about these features. For example:

> What was the poet's home like when she was a child…?

or

> Compare the poets different attitudes to their religions

Identifying the different cultures and traditions

There are various approaches to the different cultures and traditions.

- You might have to write about someone coping in a culture which is different from the one into which they were born, and might see the verse form as part of her uncertainty:

> **My salwar kameez**
> **didn't impress the schoolfriend**
> **who sat on my bed, asking to see**
> **my weekend clothes**

The girl from Pakistan feels awkward and trapped between her family's background and her life in England. The salwar kameez represents the life she has left behind. The two sides of her life are even reflected in the layout of the lines, which are uneven and fragmented...

- You might have to write about the way a society deals with its cultures and traditions, and may decide to stress the way language is used:

> **if**
> **a toktaboot**
> **thi trooth**
> **lik wanna yoo**
> **scruff yi**
> **widna thingk**
> **it wuz troo.**

The man is speaking in a Scottish accent, and the spelling, along with vocabulary, illustrates the fact that he is not part of the world of standard English. He seems an outsider, and is suggesting that only those who speak "properly" can influence others in Britain...

- You might be writing about a particular place and its problems:

> **They picked Akanni up one morning**
> **Beat him soft like clay**
> **And stuffed him down the belly**
> **Of a waiting jeep**

We are presented with a picture of life in a repressive African state, where brutal treatment is handed out, presumably by the military, and ordinary people are consumed by the state, ending up beaten and in "the belly" of a jeep...

The style of your answer

Usually, when writing about poems, it is best to follow a set pattern:

- make a point
- prove it
- explain it
- make a comparison.

For example:

The poet begins by making the reader laugh: **point**

"Excuse me
standing on one leg
I'm half-caste" **proof**

Since he is going on to explain the ridiculous way people regard "half-castes", the visual image with which he begins serves him well. **explanation**

Of course, this contrasts with the opening of... **comparison**

This technique is likely to be useful whether you are writing about content, structure or language.

The structure of your response

You will have relatively little time to write about all the things which are relevant. Consider using a simple structure which is suitable for any response requiring detailed comparison, for example, when you have a stem question followed by a series of bullets:

1. brief introduction – which poems you have chosen and why
2. a section dealing with one of the poems
3. a section dealing with the other poem **but** including comparative references to the first poem, where appropriate
4. a conclusion, summarising the similarities and/or differences.

You can vary this approach, but ensure you are **comparing** the poems, not just writing about each one separately. For instance, you could integrate your ideas:

- compare the language of each poem
- compare the social conditions detailed in each poem

and so on.

How effects are achieved

Although the implied emphasis is upon the fact that the poems are from or about different cultures and traditions, it is not enough to simply detail the content of the poetry. To do well in the exam, you still need to stress **how** the poets achieve their effects. This means you will be analysing the verse and employing the vocabulary associated with poetry:

simile	dissonance	free verse
metaphor	enjambement	refrain
alliteration	rhyme	stanza
onomatopoeia	rhythm	
assonance	symbol	

and so on.

Ideally, you should be showing how such features contribute to the message of the poem.

I remember the night my mother
was stung by a scorpion. Ten hours
of steady rain had driven him
to crawl beneath a sack of rice.
Parting with his poison – flash
of diabolic tail in the dark room –
he risked the rain again.

We are presented with a vivid picture of life in this village: rain, rice and scorpions. The attack itself appears rapid (there is the alliteration of "s"s in "stung by a scorpion"), yet it is as if the devil himself has been, with just a flash of metaphorically "diabolic tail" and a puncturing of alliterated "p"s ("parting with his poison"). The use of the enjambement, when "flash" hangs on the end of the line, gives the incident prominence, as if it is some kind of defining moment.

Then, when the scorpion heads back outside, we can almost hear the hiss of water in the alliterated phrase "risked the rain". The internal rhyme ("rain again") makes it seem as if this happens often and this downpour tends to last.

Although the attack seems so frightening, the matter-of-fact way the poet describes it in the first two lines also gives the impression that this is simply what life was like...

Poems from different cultures and traditions (1–4)

1 **(a)** In the extract below, from *Peasant Woman* by Anna Swir, explain what we learn about the woman's life. (5)

(b) How is language used to make the message clear? Find 7 examples and explain them. (7)

> She carries on her shoulders
> the house, the garden, the farm,
> the cows, the pigs, the calves, and the children.
>
> Her back wonders
> why it doesn't break.
> Her hands wonder
> why they don't fall off.
> She doesn't wonder.
>
> Like a bloodstained stick
> her dead mother's drudgery
> sustains her...

2 *Peasant Woman* is about life in Poland; *Bwalla the Hunter* – below – is set in Australia.

(a) What is similar about the two lifestyles? (2)

(b) What linguistic and poetic techniques are used to make us sympathise with Bwalla the Hunter and his family? (6)

> From *Bwalla the Hunter* by Kath Walker
>
> In the hard famine time, in the long drought
> Bwalla the hunter on walkabout,
> Lubra and children following slow,
> All proper hungry long time now.
>
> No more kangaroo out on the plain,
> Gone to other country where there was rain.
> Couldn't find emu, couldn't find seed,
> And the children all time cry for feed...

ANSWERS & TUTORIALS

SCORE

1 (a) She is responsible for providing for her family (1) and looking after the house and farm. (1) She works extremely hard (1) but knows she has to do the job. (1) She is driven on by the knowledge that her mother suffered in the same way. (1)

(b) 'She carries on her shoulders': metaphor, implying that the weight of what she carries is heavy, but she manages. (1) 'the house, the garden, the farm…': list, stressing the many demands upon her. (1) 'Her back wonders… Her hands wonder…': metaphors, implying that every part of her body is pained and complaining. (1) 'She doesn't wonder': short contrasting sentence to illustrate it is all clear to her. (1) 'Like a bloodstained stick': simile that suggests her mother was beaten. (1) Final three lines: enjambement, suggesting that the suffering of their lives drags on. (1) 'dead mother's drudgery': alliteration with depressing 'd' sounds. (1)

Avoid the temptation to write about what we are not told: here, for example, we might wonder what has happened to her husband, but do not linger over the point. Instead, concentrate on what the poet has actually written and how it has been expressed.

2 (a) The people are suffering because their lives are so hard. (1) In both cases, the children are mentioned as a major concern. (1)

(b) Sense of lasting suffering, with 'long' repeated. (1) The poem is not in standard English, and we can hear the way they talk: 'all proper hungry long time now'. (1) The rhythm of the verse is slow, like their steps: 'Lubra and children following slow'. (1) Repetition suggests emptiness: 'Couldn't find emu, couldn't find seed'. (1) Simple rhyme scheme – aabb – demonstrates the simplicity of their existence. (1) Emotive language at end: 'children all time cry for feed'. (1)

Reading this poem out loud helps you understand how the verse is intended to work. Even in an exam, it is often worthwhile reading the lines through in your head, as if you were delivering them to a hall full of people. It changes verse from a cold subject for study into a form which has real meaning; and if you can capture that emotion in your answer, you will be rewarded by the examiner.

TOTAL

What is expected

In the AQA/A Anthology, there are 16 poems from different cultures and traditions. These are divided into two clusters. You might be studying both clusters, or just one.

On the exam paper, there will be two questions on poems from different cultures, and you will choose which **one** you wish to answer. There will be one question on each cluster. If, therefore, you have studied just one cluster, you will have to answer the question which has been set on it.

You will have **45 minutes** to answer the question, and it will be on **two poems**. One of the poems will always be named; and you will have to decide which other poem is appropriate to write about, depending on the question. Since you will not know which poem will be named, it means you have to be prepared to answer on all the poems in the cluster. If you have studied poems from both clusters, though, you can write about a poem from each one in your response, if you wish.

For the **2004 exam**, you will be allowed to take an annotated Anthology into the exam, though annotations must be brief. Notes in complete sentences are not allowed: you should just use words and phrases. **After 2004**, you will be given a clean copy of the Anthology to use in the exam (though you will be allowed to make annotations during the exam). If you do annotate in the exam, you might consider quick underlining and the briefest of notes, because time is short and you have a lot to write. If you take five minutes to decide how you will answer the question, you have just 20 minutes on each poem, and will have to compare them as part of your answer.

Since you have to answer on two poems, it is useful to revise them in pairs. Because of their styles and subject matters, it is relatively straightforward to see which ones can be linked easily.

How to find links

As you read through the poems, consider linking them through what they have to say about:

- people
- situations
- politics
- change
- traditions
- differences in cultures

or through their use of:

- non-standard English
- imagery
- description
- narrative

or through the style of the poetry – how it is laid out on the page, or how rhythm and rhyme are used, or the kind of narrative voice employed, or whatever.

Here are some examples of which poems you might decide to study together:

Coming to terms with a different situation	*Presents from my Aunts in Pakistan* and *Hurricane Hits England*
Differences within societies	*Nothing's Changed* and *Two Scavengers in a Truck*
Life in very different surroundings	*Blessing* and *Night of the Scorpion* and *Island Man*
Outsiders	*From Unrelated Incidents* and *Half-Caste*
Mistreatment	*Limbo* and *Nothing's Changed* and *Not my Business*
Language	*From Search for My Tongue* and *From Unrelated Incidents*
Everyday problems overcome	*Night of the Scorpion* and *Blessing*

Remember that whatever the question, you are likely to end up writing about the message in the poems, the structure and the linguistic techniques used. So, for instance, if you were explaining how *Not my Business* and *What Were They Like?* present depressing pictures of how people have been made to suffer, you would deal with the content of the poems, but also mention how the form of the verse contributes to the effect, and how language has been used to touch the reader's emotions.

How to achieve a high grade

The grade you receive for your poetry analysis and comparison depends on how well you fulfil the requirements in the mark scheme. Obviously, much more is expected of you for higher grades.

Grade	Skills descriptors
F	• some simple comment • reference to appropriate detail • statement on some aspects of presentation
C	• effective supporting use of textual detail • some cross-reference • awareness of authorial techniques and purpose • understanding of feelings, attitudes, ideas
A	• references integrated with argument • analysis of variety of writers' techniques • exploration of and empathy with writer's ideas and attitudes

F Grade: Answers will be straightforward and will refer to the poems, but will make obvious and limited comments and interpretations, for example, 'The poem says ... and this means that the poet thinks ...'. There are likely to be references to linguistic features, but comment on them will lack depth, and they are unlikely to be seen as part of the poet's attempt to lead the reader to greater understanding: 'There is a simile, which says ...'.

C Grade: The meaning of the poem will be explained, and proof will be offered: 'The poet clearly thinks that ... because in the second stanza it says ...'. The poems will be linked: 'This is not so in the second poem, where ...'. Candidates will know what the poet is trying to achieve and will understand his or her viewpoint: 'We know the poet is angry when he writes ...'.

A Grade: Candidates will have internalised the meanings, so that they can be explained using their own words alongside the words of the poet: 'The family has been destroyed, and when the poet says ..., we sense his despair'. Responses at this level will also deal with subtleties in interpretation, will analyse what the poet says and why, rather than describing it, and try to come to terms with the poet's emotions.

A high-quality response

Here is an example of a high-quality response to a typical question:

> Explain how a different culture is presented in *Night of the Scorpion* by Nissim Ezekiel and one other poem.

Opening:

In *Night of the Scorpion*, the reader is given a picture of life in a village community in the Third World, where scorpions are a threat, medicine is not available and people must cope. There is, though, belief in God and a sense of community. *Limbo* also presents suffering, but here there are slaves who dream of a better future, where 'the music is saving me...'. They are not supported by a community, but oppressed by a whip...

This introduction links the title to the poems, and the poems to each other. We expect *Night of the Scorpion* will be examined in terms of danger, belief and a simple but supportive society. Analysis of *Limbo* might focus on what happens to the slaves, their sufferings and hopes.

Middle:

...Finally, religion performs its magic, because Ezekiel writes:

'I watched the holy man perform his rites
to tame the poison with incantation...'

Similarly, in *Limbo* the 'dumb gods' raise the beaten slaves, and the poem has the rhythm of the dance, which might represent the white man's tune, to which the slaves must dance; or could be the rhythm of their homes, still beating in their veins...

The candidate again links the poems effectively, integrating quotations and moving from description to analysis, looking at different interpretations of *Limbo*.

Ending:

...The poems, therefore, present very different pictures of life in these cultures. *Limbo* gives us slaves, darkness, violent repression, but the hope of final salvation; *Night of the Scorpion* is grounded in the present rather than the past, and shows how villagers cope positively with a problem:

'Thank God the scorpion picked on me
and spared my children.'

Once again, the comparative element is clear. This is a balanced and summative conclusion.

Poetry anthology for AQA/A (1–4)

1 What do these two extracts tell us about men who are in situations which seem less than ideal? (8)

2 How do they use verse and language to achieve their effects? (12)

I back from the glass,
boy again,
leaving small mean O
of small, mean mouth.
Hands burn
for a stone, a bomb,
to shiver down the glass.
Nothing's changed.

Tatamkhulu Afrika, writing about life in South Africa, and describing his feelings when looking into a 'whites only inn'.

Morning
and island man wakes up
to the sound of blue surf
in his head...
...Comes back to sands
of a grey metallic roar
to surge of wheels
to dull North Circular roar

muffling muffling
his crumpled pillow waves
island man heaves himself

Another London day

Grace Nichols, writing about a Caribbean island man living in London

ANSWERS & TUTORIALS

SCORE

1 Afrika feels as though he does not control his life ('boy again'). (1) He feels powerless and deprived ('small, mean mouth'). (1) Like a child, he wants to take revenge, (1) though in this case, he would mean a bomb through the window, not a stone. (1)

In contrast, Nichols tells us about Island Man's dreams, (1) contrasting them with the reality of his life in London. (1) Instead of surf, he is surrounded by the city sounds; (1) and, although he does not have Afrika's anger, he is not happy, because he 'heaves himself' into the grimness of 'another London day'. (1)

The full poems obviously have much more to offer. However, even here 'in contrast' is a vital link: you need to show the examiner you can deal with poems as a pair, rather than individually. Similarly, the phrase 'although he does not have Afrika's anger' pulls the ideas together.

2 The verse in Afrika's poem looks compact on the page, squashed like his emotions, (1) and compacted into a brief last line: 'Nothing's changed'; (1) whereas Nichol's poem has more vibrancy, one line stretching out like a wave ('to surge of wheels'). (1) However, Island Man is still depressed, emphasised by the last heavy line: 'Another London day'. (1)

The 'b' sounds in Afrika's verse suggest violence in him. (1) He repeats 'small mean' to stress his emotions. (1) There is passion in the metaphor which tells us he wants to destroy what is there ('hands burn'); (1) and onomatopoeia, as we already hear the window shattering ('shiver). (1)

Nichols' poem, on the other hand, begins more softly, with a yawned 'morning', (1) and enjambements in the first lines make us feel he is stretching pleasantly. (1) These lines contrast with more abrasive sounds later as he wakes fully ('grey metallic'), (1) though they are still mixed with the sounds of the sea ('soar', 'surge'), until his dream is gone, stressed by the repetition 'muffling muffling'. (1)

Quality responses will make close reference to the texts and be able to use appropriate vocabulary effectively.

TOTAL

What is expected

The pre-release booklet for AQA/B will include between eight and ten poems from different cultures and traditions. Your understanding of such poetry will be tested on Paper 2, and you will have 45 minutes to write about **one** of the poems and **another** which you have not seen before and which will be printed on the paper.

This means you must:

- prepare the poems which are provided in advance, know what they have to say and how the poets convey their ideas
- be ready to deal with an unseen poem, and be able to examine it in terms of message, structure and language.

You will probably be faced with a stem question, asking you to compare a pre-prepared poem with the unseen one, and a series of bullets asking more precise questions. Although the structure of the questions could vary, the likely approach is:

- two bullets on the unseen poem
- a third bullet asking you to compare some aspect of it with the pre-release poem.

> For example:
>
> Compare *Bwalla the Hunter*, from the pre-release material, with *Beggar* by Murano Shiro.
>
> - What impression of the man is created in *Beggar*?
> - How is language in *Beggar* used to convey the poet's ideas?
> - What are the similarities and differences between the lives of the beggar and Bwalla the Hunter?

You should therefore study the pre-release poems for what they contain, but you can also use them as general preparation for dealing with an unseen poem on the day of the exam.

At least one part of the question will require you to write about some feature of different cultures (family, society, politics or whatever), but since that is likely to be central to the poem or poems anyway, you will just be dealing with some of the meaning. There is no need to worry about it being an extra element. So, for instance, in the example above, you deal with it when writing about 'the lives of…'.

How to achieve a high grade

Avoid the temptation to generalise in your answer or to assume the examiner knows the answer so that you do not need to be precise. Ground your ideas in what the poems have to say and quote appropriately.

Even at the **bottom** of the mark range, examiners are expecting:

- clear understanding
- relevant quotation
- explanations of how language is used
- some interpretation of the poems' ideas.

For **higher grades**, you will have to demonstrate:

- a detailed and subtle understanding and interpretation of the poems
- the ability to select references which are focused and precise
- the ability to make cross-references between the poems
- a detailed, critical evaluation of how the writers use language.

Remember, too, to make direct comparisons, rather than juxtaposing ideas – do not just put them side by side and expect the examiner to make the connections. This answer, for example, makes direct comparisons:

> The beggar's life seems totally miserable. We are told he "trails" his soul behind, and is "like an unhappy child". The simile gives the tragic impression of a schoolboy dragging himself from an unhappy home to an oppressive school.
>
> Although Bwalla and his family move similarly slowly ("following slow"), the hunter is described as much more dynamic, and a very different simile is chosen to describe him. When he steals the wallaby from the eagle, he is "like a cat" and he provides food for his family. The beggar, meanwhile, is fading away, so almost all his existence seems "dissolved".

Notice that the candidate integrates quotations into the answer seamlessly, detailing and explaining the poets' ideas. The points of comparison are highlighted (slow movement/similes/attitudes) and a suitable comparative vocabulary is employed ('more dynamic'/ 'very different'/ 'meanwhile'). The meanings of the poems are interpreted and the language is analysed ('tragic impression'/ 'much more dynamic').

Poetry for AQA/B (1–2)

1 (a) What impression of life is given by Lauris Edmond in this poem from New Zealand? (3)

(b) How is language used to convey the message? (7)

> **It's barely light, and out in the tree tops**
> **cicadas already are shrieking high noon –**
>
> **how absolutely, with what high assurance,**
> **the sharp little creatures live at the heart**
>
> **of their days, wearing the weather, the daylight**
> **and dark, right up close to the skin; as though**
>
> **to be alive at all – to wake up – is to act, and**
> **to shout of it...**
>
> **From *The Heat of Summer***

2 (a) In what ways are the two people described in these poems different? (5)

(b) How do the structures of the poems add to the effect? (5)

> **Staggering down the road at midnight**
> **home from the bar, the**
>
> **mexican Bandit stood facing me, about**
> **to improve his standard of living**
>
> **Two**
> **fingers handled the moustache gently,**
> **the other hand fingered the pistol...**
>
> **From *The Encounter* by Paul Blackburn, America**

> **You were**
> **water to me**
> **deep and bold and fathoming...**
>
> **You were**
> **sunrise to me**
> **rise and warm and steaming**
>
> **You were**
> **the fishes red gill to me**
> **the flame tree's spread to me...**
>
> **From *Praise Song for my Mother* by Grace Nichols, from Guyana**

ANSWERS & TUTORIALS

SCORE

1 (a) There is a sense that exotic nature is a part of life ('cicadas'); (1) and that everything is bound closely to nature ('wearing the weather'); (1) and that life is exciting, full of possibilities ('wake up... act...shout...'). (1)

(b) Onomatopoeia captures the sounds ('shrieking') of the cicadas. (1) Everything seems sharp – represented by the alliteration of 't's in 'tree tops', (1) and by the description of the cicadas. (1) The extended sentence makes it seem that impressions are tumbling, one upon the other. (1) Metaphors illustrate how the cicadas are central to an understanding of this nature ('heart of their days', (1) 'wearing the weather'. (1) The verbs to finish give an impression of life and awakening ('to wake up... to act... to shout'). (1)

Answer 1(b) could be supplemented by mention of the enjambements and their effects, and by explanation of the other alliteration ('wearing the weather'). The important thing, though, is to note the variety of points which are present, and the need to link them through an overview of the poet's message.

2 (a) The Bandit is menacing, (1) and a stereotype, one hand stroking his moustache whilst the other is on his gun. (1) Nichols' mother, in contrast, suggests calm, and the water imagery is of life ('deep and bold and fathoming'); (1) she is an awakening ('sunrise'); (1) and she reminds her daughter of the wonders of nature ('fishes red gill ...'). (1)

(b) The broken verses of *The Encounter* reflect the drunkenness of the poet (1) and we have a narrative approach. (1) Nichols' poem, on the other hand, is lyrical, (1) and gives a series of impressions, rather than a story. (1) The repeated 'You were ...' in each regular stanza makes it seem like an incantation. (1)

In the exam, people would no doubt be linked in any question to their culture and tradition. However, details in these answers would support further explanations: the idea of bandits and America's history; and the details emerging in Nichols' poem which give a glimpse of Caribbean colour.

TOTAL

Learning spellings and spelling unknown words

If you are learning a new spelling first **LOOK** at it (to see if it reminds you of any other words or spelling patterns you already know), then **COVER** it (and try to 'see' the word in your mind's eye), then **WRITE** it (from memory) and finally **CHECK** it (to see if you were right).

If you have to spell a difficult or new word from memory or from just hearing it, **LISTEN** to its sound (say it slowly to yourself several times) and think which letters might represent those sounds; **THINK** about spelling rules or patterns you know; **WRITE** down two or three spellings which might be correct then decide which looks or 'feels' right. Finally **CHECK** in a dictionary/spellchecker.

You won't always be able to use a spellchecker or a dictionary or ask someone how to spell a word, especially in an exam. So learn to:

- think about word families: if you can spell *appear*, you shouldn't have problems with *disappear, disappearing, disappeared*, and so on;
- think about word origins: you shouldn't forget the *n* in 'government' if you remember that its job is to *govern* us.

Spelling rules

- *q* is always followed by *u*, except in *Iraq*.
- *i* comes before *e* except when it follows *c* (e.g. *friend, brief,* but *ceiling, receive*).
- If *all* is followed by another syllable, it loses one *l* (e.g. *also, already, always*; but note that *all right* must be written as two words).
- If a word ends with a single vowel followed by a single consonant, you must double the consonant if adding an ending which begins with a vowel (e.g. *shop–shopped–shopping*; *swim–swimmer–swimming*).
- If you add *full* or *till* to the end of another word or syllable, you must drop one *l* (e.g. *hopeful, until*).

More spelling rules

- Drop the final *e* from a word if adding an ending which starts with a vowel (e.g. *love–loving; rattle–rattling*).
- Keep the final *e* in a word if adding an ending which begins with a consonant (e.g. *love–lovely; rattle–rattled*).
- If a word ends with a consonant followed by *y*, change the *y* to *i* before all endings except *ing* (e.g. *funny–funnily; marry–married–marrying*).
- An *i* or *ee* sound at the end of a word is nearly always shown by the letter *y* (e.g. *country, hungry*, but common exceptions are *coffee, committee* and *taxi* as well as foreign borrowings, especially Italian words such as *macaroni* and *spaghetti*).
- The *i before e except after c* rule is generally true, but not if the sound is *ay* (e.g. *neighbour* and *weigh*). Other common exceptions to this rule are: *counterfeit, foreign, forfeit, leisure, reign, seize, sovereign.*
- Think about the meanings of words which sound the same but have different spellings (e.g. *their/there/they're* and *to/too/two*).

Plurals

- **Regular** plurals are formed by simply adding an *s* to the singular word (e.g. *horse–horses; dog–dogs*).
- Words which end with a consonant followed by *y* form the plural by changing the *y* to *ies* (e.g. *baby–babies; lady–ladies*).
- To form the plural of a word ending in *s, x, z, ch, sh* or *ss*, add *es* (e.g. *bus–buses, fox–foxes, church–churches, miss–misses*).
- Most singular words which end with *f* or *fe* change the *f* or *fe* to *ves* to form the plural (e.g. *knife–knives; leaf–leaves; wife–wives*). Common exceptions to this rule are *chief, dwarf, roof* and *safe* which simply add an *s* to form their plural.
- A few words can form their plural either by adding *s* or by changing the final *f* to *ves* (e.g. *hoof; scarf; wharf*).

Spelling (1–2)

1 Which spelling rules do the following words illustrate?

(a) neighbour (1)
(b) hurried (1)
(c) making (1)
(d) already (1)
(e) deceive (1)
(f) dropped (1)
(g) retrieve (1)
(h) lovely (1)
(i) useful (1)
(j) swimming (1)

Good spelling is seen as an important social skill

2 Check that you know the following spellings by using the LOOK – COVER – WRITE – CHECK technique:

(a) independent (1)
(b) appropriate (1)
(c) technological (1)
(d) beautiful (1)
(e) dramatically (1)

Even if you have access to a spell-checker, don't desert your dictionary!

3 What are the plural forms of the following words?

(a) baby (1)
(b) church (1)
(c) fox (1)
(d) roof (1)
(e) wharf (1)

ANSWERS & TUTORIALS

SCORE

1 Spelling rules

(a) neighbour – if the sound is *ay*, the *i before e* rule does not apply (1)

(b) hurried – change *y* to *i* before endings (except *ing*) (1)

(c) making – drop the final *e* before endings which start with a vowel (1)

(d) already – drop one *l* from *all* before another syllable (1)

(e) deceive – *e* before *i* after *c* (1)

(f) dropped – double the final consonant before adding an ending (1)

(g) retrieve – *i* before *e* except after *c* (1)

(h) lovely – keep the final *e* if adding an ending which begins with a consonant (1)

(i) useful – drop one *l* from *full* when adding it to another word (1)

(j) swimming – double the final consonant if adding an ending beginning with a vowel (1)

Find examples of words which fit these rules in your own writing. You will learn them more easily if you can remember them in a particular sentence that you have used.

2 LOOK – COVER – WRITE – CHECK

(a) independent (1)

(b) appropriate (1)

(c) technological (1)

(d) beautiful (1)

(e) dramatically (1)

These may be words that you need to use in various GCSE exams. Make sure that you learn the spellings of technical terms in each of your subjects.

3 Plural forms

(a) babies (1)

(b) churches (1)

(c) foxes (1)

(d) roofs (1)

(e) wharfs *or* wharves (1)

TOTAL

Sentences

Basic sentence punctuation requires an upper case (or capital) letter at the start and a full stop at the end. Longer sentences may need commas, semi-colons, colons, exclamation or question marks.

In *Lord of the Flies*, William Golding writes:

> **He was old enough, twelve years and a few months, to have lost the prominent tummy of childhood; and not yet old enough for adolescence to have made him awkward.**

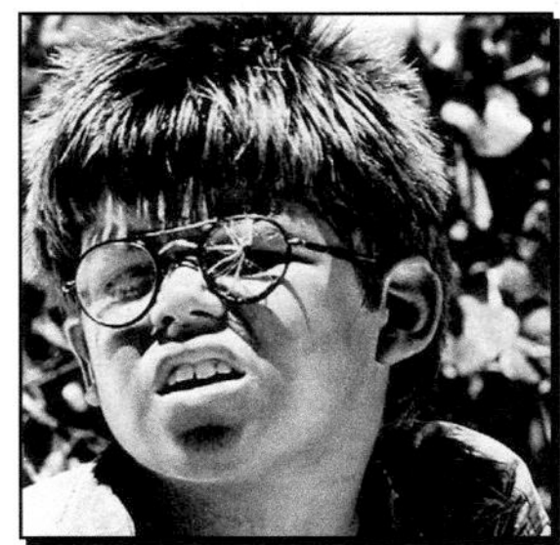

Because the sentence contains two definite ideas – contrasting childhood and adolescence – they have been separated with a semi-colon. This shows a sophisticated grasp of sentence structure and punctuation. It is better than writing two separate sentences as the ideas are closely linked. The commas in this example are used to separate a descriptive phrase (which adds to the meaning, but is not indispensable) from the main sentence.

The other main use of commas is to separate a list, as in this example from Harper Lee's *To Kill a Mockingbird*:

> **Of all days Sunday was the day for formal afternoon visiting: ladies wore corsets, men wore coats, children wore shoes.**

This example also shows the most frequent use of the colon, which is to introduce a list.

Question marks must be put at the end of direct questions. **Exclamation marks** indicate strong emotions such as anger or astonishment as well as humour. Remember that well-chosen words will convey emotion too, and do not rely on exclamation marks alone to affect your reader's response!

Punctuating speech

Another passage from *Lord of the Flies* illustrates the main rules.

> **'I don't care what they call me,' he said confidentially, 'so long as they don't call me what they used to call me at school.'**
>
> **Ralph was faintly interested.**
>
> **'What was that?'**
>
> **The fat boy glanced over his shoulder, then leaned towards Ralph.**
>
> **He whispered.**
>
> **'They used to call me "Piggy".'**

Note that you should:

- put all the words spoken inside speech marks;
- begin each new piece of speech with a capital letter unless it is the continuation of a sentence (as in Piggy's opening remark);
- place punctuation of the spoken words inside the speech marks (e.g. the comma after 'me' in the first line, and the question mark at the end of Ralph's query);
- use double speech marks inside the normal single speech marks for a title or nickname, as in the last line above.

Apostrophes

These have two functions:

- to show missing letters in abbreviated words such as *wasn't* (was not), *can't* (cannot), *I've* (I have) and so on. The apostrophe is placed where the missing letters would be.
- to show possession (e.g. *the boy's coat, the women's partners*).

Remember that *it's* means *it is* (e.g. *it's very hot in here*); *its* means *belonging to it*, as in *the dog chased its ball.*

Punctuation (1–2)

1 Insert two commas and two semi-colons in this sentence from *Turned* by Charlotte Perkins Gilman: (4)

> **She sobbed bitterly chokingly despairingly her shoulders heaved and shook convulsively her hands were tight-clenched.**

2 Insert the missing punctuation into this passage from *The Darkness Out There* by Penelope Lively: (16)

> **The door opened Kerry said wherell I put the clippings theres the compost heap down the bottom by the fence and while youre down there could you get some sticks from the wood for kindling theres a good lad**

SCORE

1 In the original the punctuation is:

She sobbed bitterly, (1) chokingly, (1) despairingly; (1) her shoulders heaved and shook convulsively; (1) her hands were tight-clenched.

There are no alternatives possible here; the commas separate a list of adverbs and the semi-colons separate the three parts of the sentence – which describe the woman's sobbing, then her shoulders, then her hands.

2 In the original the punctuation is:

The door opened. (1) Kerry said, (1) '(1)Where'll (2) I put the clippings?(1)'

'(1)There's (2) the compost heap down the bottom, (1) by the fence. (1) And (1) while you're (1) down there could you get some sticks from the wood for kindling, (1) there's (1) a good lad (1).'

Note only one mark is given for each pair of speech marks. Two marks are given in each case for *Where'll* and *There's* as each requires a capital letter and an apostrophe.

An allowable alternative would be to put a comma after 'fence', a small 'a' for 'and', and another comma after 'there'.

If you start a passage of direct speech with a phrase such as 'Kerry said', you must put a comma after these words and before the speech marks – but remember to start the spoken words with a capital letter. Here is another example from *Salt on the Snow* by Rukshana Smith:

Rashmi pointed to the ceiling and Julie said, 'Not where, how?'

TOTAL

Formal writing

You may well be asked to produce a piece of formal writing in your examination. In formal writing you must choose your words more carefully and precisely than you would if making casual notes or if in conversation with a friend. Consider this sentence from *Birdsong* by Sebastian Faulks:

> **The town side of the boulevard backed on to substantial gardens which were squared off and apportioned with civic precision to the houses they adjoined.**

Note how the writer conveys the impression that this street is inhabited by well-off and important (perhaps even self-important), orderly and conventional people. All of this is done by using words such as 'substantial', 'squared off', 'apportioned', 'civic', 'precision' and 'adjoined'. Not a word is wasted in suggesting the characters of the inhabitants before you have actually met them. Even the use of 'houses' rather than *homes* implies rather cold or unemotional people. Think how little you would be able to speculate about them if the author had simply written, *The houses on the town side of the boulevard had large, neat gardens*. There is nothing 'flashy' about this writing: merely well-chosen words which, together, give a clear viewpoint and invite some speculation.

Informal writing

You might have the opportunity to write less formally in the examination. For instance, you could be expected to write a letter to a friend or an article for a teenage magazine. That could mean it would be appropriate to use slang (for example, 'kids' instead of 'children') or even a completely different style or approach: 'Don't diss me, man...' However, although examiners welcome a targeted approach to the purpose and audience, you will still be expected to demonstrate a wide range of vocabulary and an ability to write in sentences, to spell correctly and use paragraphs effectively.

Details

Whatever you are writing, remember that precise and appropriate use of detail is a key to success. The examiner will react more positively to a point which you have proved, or to a description which comes to life, or to a point of view which appears to be supported by logic.

Consider the difference between these statements:

> **1** I think the government is stupid.
>
> **2** What annoys me most about the government is when a spokesperson comes on to the television and says something we all clearly know is wrong, such as…

Even if the reader disagrees with the second statement, it will be clear why the writer feels this way.

Now look at these statements:

> **1** It was hot on holiday.
>
> **2** The temperature reached 36 degrees whilst we were in Spain, and grandma had to sit under the shower for hours on end…

The first statement is vague: 'hot' is an opinion which will mean different things to different people. The second statement, though, is supported factually and gives the reader an image which supports the idea.

Non-fiction texts

You need to be equally precise whether you are writing fiction or non-fiction. Your writing needs to evoke people, places, events and feelings through the vocabulary and imagery you use. Your argumentative, persuasive, advisory, informative writing and so on must be clear, to the point and sensibly structured if its purpose is to be understood and your comments and opinions are to be accepted.

Vocabulary and style (1–2)

1 Read this extract from Penelope Lively's *The Darkness Out There.* It describes a girl walking past a place where a German fighter plane had crashed during the war, killing its crew. Comment on the effectiveness of the underlined words, phrases and punctuation: (10)

> **She kept to the track, walking in the flowers with corn running in the wind between her and the spinney. She thought suddenly of blank-eyed helmeted heads, looking at you from among the branches. She wouldn't go in there for a thousand pounds, not even in bright day like now, with nothing coming out of the dark slab of trees but bird song – blackbirds and thrushes and robins and that. It was a rank place, all whippy saplings and brambles and a gully with a dumped mattress and bedstead and an old fridge. And somewhere, presumably, the crumbling rusty scraps of metal and cloth and ... bones?**

2 These lines are from *Wil Williams (1861–1910)* by Gillian Clarke.

(a) What does the description of the stations tell you about what happened to them and why? (3)

(b) How do the last two lines convey an air of sadness? (3)

> **The stations with their cabbage-patches**
> **and tubbed geraniums are closed**
> **and the trains' long cries are swallowed**
> **in the throats of the tunnels.**

3 What is particularly effective about these two lines from Bill Bryson's *Notes from a Small Island*? (4) It describes part of a train journey in Wales.

> The towns along the way all had names that sounded like a cat bringing up a hairball: Llywyngwril, Morfa Mawddach, Llandecwyn, Dyffryn Ardudwy.

ANSWERS & TUTORIALS

SCORE

1 'Running' conveys both an image of the movement of the corn in the wind (1) but also suggests the girl's fear and her own instincts to run past this spooky place. (1)
'Dark slab of trees' suggests a threatening presence because of the word 'dark', (1) while 'slab' may make you think of a body at the undertaker's. (1)
'Rank' appeals to your sense of smell and emphasises the unpleasantness of the place. (1) It is also suggestive of the war (i.e. 'rank' as in ranks of soldiers). (1)
'Whippy' again conveys a sense of movement and threat. (1) It also suggests the idea of punishment. (1)
'...' is used to make you stop and think (1) and so build up the air of suspense. (1)

2 **(a)** They have been turned into houses, (1) with vegetables (1) and flowers (1) growing in the gardens.
(b) The last two lines convey an air of sadness:
- through the reference to swallowing and the throats of tunnels, as in swallowing back tears; (1)
- the fact that the tunnels are no longer used by trains; (1)
- the description of the noise once made by the trains as crying. (1)

3 The image is effective because it is unexpected (1) and both humorous (1) and slightly disgusting; (1) it makes the reader think carefully about the Welsh place-names. (1)

All these examples show you how effective single words, images and punctuation can be in your writing. Keep thinking about the **purpose** of what you are writing and the effect you wish to have on your **audience**.

LLYWYNGWRIL

MORFA MAWDDACH

LLANDECWYN

DYFFRYN ARDUDWY

TOTAL

Your response to other people's writing, and the style of your own writing, must take account of its intended purpose and its target audience. This means thinking about formality and informality in your use of language. For example, think about how you might aid characterisation by using non-standard forms of English in dialogue in a story. Also important is the extent to which you can show your knowledge of, and control over, a range of different sentence structures.

Note the effective contrast in this extract from Barry Hines' *A Kestrel for a Knave* between informal, non-standard English in the spoken words to the formality and variety in the descriptive writing:

> **'It was a funny feeling though when he'd gone; all quiet, with nobody there, and up to t'knees in tadpoles.'**
>
> **Silence. The class up to their knees in tadpoles. Mr Farthing allowed them a pause for assimilation. Then, before their involvement could disintegrate into local gossip, he used it to try to inspire an emulator.**

Showing a range of techniques

If you can vary the structures of your own writing, you are likely to gain a high grade in your examination. The aim is not only to show your skill in varying sentence structures, but to match them to the needs of the moment. Barry Hines does this by gradually lengthening the sentences. This reflects the tension of the moment, which the teacher tries to capture and maintain.

In writing fiction, then, make the sentence structures play their part in creating mood and conveying atmosphere. Look at this passage from William Golding's *Lord of the Flies*:

> **Wave after wave, Ralph followed the rise and fall until something of the remoteness of the sea numbed his brain. Then gradually the almost infinite size of this water forced itself on his attention. This was the divider, the barrier. On the other side of the island, swathed at midday with mirage, defended by the shield of the quiet lagoon, one might dream of rescue; but here, faced by the brute obtuseness of the ocean, the miles of division, one was clamped down, one was helpless, one was condemned, one was –**

The rhythm of the opening words in the Golding extract reflects the movement of the sea itself. Then the long, unfinished sentence mirrors the difficult nature of the idea with which Ralph is grappling. The mounting panic in his mind is mirrored in the repetitive structure of the closing phrases. Long sentences, carefully used, can be most effective. Combined with the use of the present tense, this technique can give immediacy and forcefulness to writing, especially in a piece of non-fiction. As an example of this, read this extract from *Hong Kong* by Jan Morris:

> I leave my typewriter for a moment, open the sliding glass doors and walk out to the balcony; and away from the hotel's insulated stillness, instantly like the blast of history itself the frantic noise of Hong Kong hits me, the roar of that traffic, the thumping of that jack-hammer, the chatter of a million voices across the city below; and once again the smell of greasy duck and gasoline reaches me headily out of China.

Note the use of semi-colons by both William Golding and Jan Morris. This adds to the effects achieved by both writers in building sweeping sentences which carry the reader along on a flood of ideas and descriptive details.

Another way of achieving immediacy is by using 'ungrammatical' sentences. For example, this is how Dylan Thomas begins *The Outing: A Story*:

> **If you can call it a story. There's no real beginning or end and there's very little in the middle.**

Sentence structures (1–2)

1 Join the following sentences into one: (4)

He was carrying a foolish wooden stick.
The boar was only five yards away.
He flung the stick.
He saw it hit the great snout.
It hung there for a moment.

2 Comment on the effects achieved by the sentence structures in this extract from *By Desert Ways to Baghdad* by Louisa Jebb: (6)

> Last night we were dirty, isolated, and free, tonight we are clean, sociable and trammelled.
>
> Last night the setting sun's final message written in flaming signs of gold was burnt into us, and the starry heights carried our thoughts heavenward and made them free as ourselves. Tonight the sunset passed all unheeded and we gaze, as we retire from the busy rush of the trivial day, at a never-ending, twisting, twirling pattern on the four walls that imprison us, oppressed by the confining ceiling of our room in the Damascus Palace Hotel.

3 Read this extract from Blake Morrison's *And when did you last see your father?*, in which he describes his father's death from cancer. How do the sentence structures contribute to the feelings he conveys? Think about the grammar and the stylistic features used. (10)

> **Midwinter half-light. The hardest frost of the year, and everything has ground to a halt, the ponds frozen, the trees under arrest, the canal locks locked. The sun can do nothing about this. It lies all day on its bed of hills, then sinks red-faced behind Pendle. It can't get up. It can't get up.**

ANSWERS & TUTORIALS

SCORE

1 The example is taken from William Golding's *Lord of the Flies*, where the sentence actually reads:

> **With the boar only five yards away, he flung the foolish wooden stick that he carried, saw it hit the great snout and hang there for a moment.**

You are unlikely to have come up with precisely this, but award youself 1 mark for each successful join in the sentences. (4)

2 The opening sentence uses repetition of structure (1) to highlight the contrast between last night and tonight. (1) The other two sentences develop this technique (1) by expanding details about last night and tonight into one sentence each. (1)
The three sentences gradually become longer, (1) which reflects the writer's sense of frustration at being 'imprisoned' within the decorative fussiness of the hotel room. (1)
Always look for structural patterns and repeats such as this in the work of other writers. Think about how you might use them in your own writing. If you are describing contrasts of any kind, repetitive sentence structures in which you change crucial details are highly effective in drawing a reader's attention to the ideas you wish to convey.

3 The first sentence is 'ungrammatical' (1) and gains your attention by making a bare statement about the setting. (1) The repetition in the second sentence, (1) together with the extended metaphor (1) and the pun on 'lock', (1) emphasises the severity of the weather. (1) The personification of the sun (1) reflects the writer's own feelings of helplessness. (1) The repetition of the final sentences (1) makes the reader aware that the description has really been about the writer's father as much as the weather. (1)

TOTAL

When you plan your own writing, you must have an overview of the whole text – not only its content, but how it moves from the beginning to the end in a way which will engage readers.

When you have finished a piece of writing, you must check and revise it to ensure that the overall structure and effect is what you intended. Careful planning will help greatly. This means thinking about the content of different sections of the text (such as paragraphs), the progress from one section to another, and the beginning and end in particular.

Paragraphs

These organise meaning and make your text accessible to the reader. A paragraph will usually be one or more sentences which are connected by:

- *topic or subject* – perhaps a character or setting in a story, or one aspect of the idea or argument in a non-fiction text;
- *narrative or chronological sequence* (e.g. the stages of a journey made by a character in a story or the order of instructions for assembling a piece of furniture);
- *an argument or approach* (e.g. reasons why you do or don't believe in ghosts in a piece of writing about the supernatural).

Use paragraphs flexibly. They do not have to be so many lines or so many sentences long. Variety in paragraph length – just as in sentence structures – can contribute to the tone or atmosphere you are trying to create. Look at the extract from *Examination Day* by Henry Slesar (overleaf). A boy in a future society is about to undergo an intelligence test to decide if he is allowed to survive or not. The tension is created by each event being in a separate paragraph.

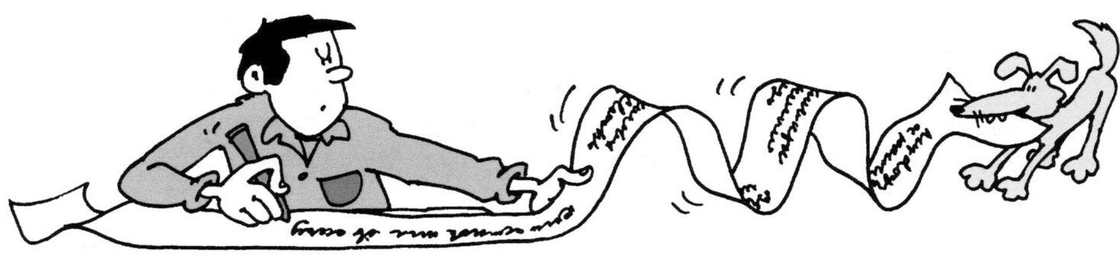

Use paragraphs flexibly.

A concealed loudspeaker crackled and called off the first name.
Dickie saw a boy leave his father's side reluctantly and walk slowly towards the door.
At five minutes of eleven, they called the name of Jordan.
'Good luck, son,' his father said, without looking at him. 'I'll call for you when the test is over.'

Beginnings and endings

Opening paragraphs need to grab your reader's attention. Use them to state an idea boldly, to introduce a memorable character, to start a dialogue which sets up a conflict, or to intrigue your reader with something unusual. This is how Margaret Atwood starts *The Big Man*:

Julie broke up with Connor in the middle of a swamp.

Endings need plenty of thought as well. You can do various things with an ending. You might neatly round off a story, as Penelope Lively does in *The Darkness Out There*:

She walked behind him, through a world grown unreliable, in which flowers sparkle and birds sing but everything is not as it appears, oh no.

Or you can try the more risky, but often effective, technique of leaving the reader wondering and wanting more. This is how Charlotte Perkins Gilman ends *Turned*:

He looked from one to the other dumbly.
And the woman who had been his wife asked quietly:
'What have you to say to us?'

It would be disastrous to leave your reader high and dry in a piece of non-fiction writing, especially if it is instructional in any way. Once again, remember to test your approach against the demands of **purpose** and **audience**.

Structuring whole texts (1–2)

1 Identify the kind of writing for which each of the following might be a suitable beginning, (5) and explain why: (5)

(i) The body was found, the dagger planted deep in its back, in the windowless, locked drawing-room, with the key jammed in the key-hole on the inside.
(ii) 'Oh Joe', she sighed, 'we're always going to be so happy!'
(iii) Before you start, make sure that you have identified all the fittings and that the necessary tools are to hand.
(iv) Do you really believe that foxes enjoy being torn apart by a pack of hounds?
(v) I hadn't expected the Bishop to be wearing a dress, fishnet tights and a lopsided grin when he opened the door.

2 The following are actual endings from books. What kind of book do you think each is, and why? (10)

(i) 'I've had enough of Nakhodka,' Wanda said. Her teeth were chattering. 'It's a hell of a place. What's more I've had enough of Siberia, and we've all had enough of Mischa, and I'm fed up with your damn maps. I want to go home.' So we did.
(ii) I signalled the bus-driver and he stopped the bus for me right outside the cottage, and I flew down the steps of the bus straight into the arms of the waiting mother.
(iii) When he arrived home there was no one in. He buried the hawk in the field just behind the shed; went in, and went to bed.
(iv) As scientists and humanists doctors will be needed to help to provide the answers, a task – to return to George Eliot – that will certainly 'call forth the highest intellectual strain'.
(v) The photograph was still there. He was for a moment surprised that Dalgleish hadn't taken it. But then he remembered. It didn't matter. There would be no trial now, no exhibits, no need to produce it as evidence in court. It wasn't needed any more. It was of no importance. He left it on the table and, turning to join Kate, walked with her in silence to the car.

SCORE

1 **(i)** A detective/whodunnit/mystery story (1) which makes you want to know how the crime was committed. (1)

(ii) A romance (1) which might be serious or not/happy or not – you want to know more about the characters. (1)

(iii) A set of instructions (1) which ensures that the reader is properly prepared for the task. (1)

(iv) A piece of argumentative writing/polemic (a powerful, one-sided argument) (1) which makes you question your own beliefs/attitudes. (1)

(v) Probably a humorous story, possibly a mystery, (1) which is so bizarre in the picture it conjures up that you want to know more. (1)

You will probably write more subtly than in these examples, but they illustrate how easily you can set up expectations in your readers.

2 **(i)** A travel book (*The Big Red Train Ride* by Eric Newby) (1) – the clues are in the place-names and the reference to going home. (1)

(ii) An autobiography (Roald Dahl's *Going Solo*) (1) – the clue is the reference to mother. (1)
This is less obvious than the previous example – it could conceivably have been the end of a novel or short story.

(iii) A novel (*A Kestrel for a Knave* by Barry Hines) (1) – the clue is that it is clearly part of a narrative. (1)

(iv) A non-fiction text (Alan Norton, *Drugs, Science and Society*) (1) – the clue is in the references to scientists/doctors and the fact that this is clearly the end of presenting an argument of some sort. (1)

(v) A detective story (*Original Sin* by P. D. James) (1) – the clue is in the references to trial, exhibits and court. (1)

TOTAL

Your written work cannot achieve its full effect on the reader (especially if that reader is an examiner) unless you present it **neatly** and **clearly**. Depending on the kind or genre of writing it is, it may also be helpful to use a range of suitable presentational devices to break up the text.

Handwriting

However much you like to use computers for coursework, you will have to handwrite your examination papers. Try to develop handwriting which uses CLUES:

- Consistently shaped and joined letters
- Letters – clear distinction between upper (capital) and lower (small) case
- Upright, or at least always leans in the same direction
- Evenly spaced
- Sensible size – neither too cramped nor too spread out.

Consider what you use to write with – the correct pen for you (in terms of diameter, balance, weight and so on) will improve both the speed and quality of your handwriting.

Breaking up the text

If writing prose fiction, remember to use **paragraphs** (page 75). You might also use chapter headings in a longer story. You could use titles in a sequence of poems, which may be broken up into stanzas (or verses). Scripts for media such as stage, radio, film or television need to follow appropriate layout conventions regarding stage/camera directions, set details and so on.

If you are writing non-fiction, remember that you can use a **range of devices** – including titles, underlinings, different margin sizes/ indentations, headings and subheadings, frames, bullet points and numbered instructions. All of these can be done by hand in an examination, where appropriate.

Titles, charts and diagrams may also make your meaning clearer, but may be less easy to produce without IT. Do not try to use a range of colours on your examination paper, as this may cause confusion for markers and checkers at a later stage. In fact, many examination boards instruct you to use only blue or black ink in their answer books.

Editing and proofreading

The final aspect of presentation is the last set of checks that you carry out in an examination. **Editing** means looking back over the work you have written and asking yourself the following questions:

- Have I adopted the best tone/approach for the target audience, using a range of appropriate language and grammatical constructions?
- Have I achieved my purpose in the overall effect of the piece?
- Have I made the best choice of content in respect of audience and purpose?
- Is the structure and presentation of the piece logical, coherent and helpful?
- Is the piece easily understood and attractive to look at?

Proofreading means checking:

- spelling
- punctuation
- grammar.

Good spelling is essential as an important social skill.

Don't worry about making alterations or corrections in your work. If you do it neatly, the examiner will be impressed that you have checked your work thoroughly in the first place, and that you have been able to identify and correct errors.

Presenting written work (1–2)

1 An examination question gives you a text on the subject of under-age drinking and asks you to re-present it in an appropriate, attractive style for teenagers. Suggest six presentational devices you could employ in an examination answer, and explain the usefulness of each. (12)

2 What are the five aspects of editing you should know and use in an examination? (5)

3 What are the three aspects of proofreading you should know and use in an examination? (3)

ANSWERS & TUTORIALS

SCORE

1 Presentational devices:

(i) Title (1) to attract the reader's interest. (1)

(ii) Sub-headings (1) help to make the structure of the argument clear to readers. (1)

(iii) Bullet points (1) can clarify lists and/or emphasise important points. (1)

(iv) Diagrams (1) give an attractive appearance/appeal to less keen readers. (1)

(v) Graphs/charts/tables (1) can make statistical information/figures easier to take in. (1)

(vi) Framing and/or writing in columns (1) can break up an otherwise large area of text and make it more accessible. (1)

2 Five aspects of editing:

(i) Is the tone/approach right for the target audience? (Have I used a range of appropriate language and grammatical constructions?) (1)

(ii) Have I achieved my purpose in the overall effect of the piece? (1)

(iii) Have I made the best choice of content in respect of audience and purpose? (1)

(iv) Is the structure and presentation of the piece logical, coherent and helpful? (1)

(v) Is the piece easily understood and attractive to look at? (1)

3 Three aspects of proofreading:

- Spelling (1)
- Punctuation (1)
- Grammar (1)

TOTAL

Several specifications require you to produce writing that argues, persuades or advises.

If you are taking **AQA Specification A**, you will be offered a choice of questions. There will be four tasks, and you will respond to just **one** of them, in 45 minutes:

- Task 1: Writing to argue
- Task 2: Writing to persuade
- Task 3: Writing to advise
- Task 4: A title which will expect you to use more than one of the skills. You might, for example, have to write a letter to a relative, using persuasion or argument to advise them on some matter.

If you are taking **AQA Specification B**, there is no choice of question. There will be just one title, to which you must respond in 40 minutes. It could be asking you to argue, or persuade, or advise, or to exhibit a mixture of these skills.

Whichever examination you are taking, however, you need to be able to write in all three styles if you are to be properly prepared for any title you are given.

Argument: priorities

For an argument to be convincing, it needs to be **logical**. This means that planning must be careful and effective. An argument will require:

- an introduction
- development
- a conclusion
- discourse markers to link ideas.

In addition, to argue, there must be **opposing viewpoints**. In your writing, therefore, you must make sure that you include a viewpoint other than the one you are supporting.

Finally, there are **high-quality features** which, if included, should mean you receive a higher mark. These are found in good writing and are specified in examiners' mark schemes: things like anecdote, rhetorical language, examples, quotations and humour.

Logical development

Your argument will only be successful if readers believe what you write. If your ideas are not well structured and do not follow logically, you are unlikely to convince them. You must try to avoid the audience thinking: 'Ah, yes, but what about...?' by dealing with that point and being logical to rid them of any doubts.

There are various techniques you can use to make it seem like your ideas are perfectly sensible:

- Plan carefully, know what you are going to write and in what order, and how your piece of writing will begin and end. Knowing precisely what you believe, and exactly why you believe it, is essential before you begin your response.
- Concentrate on paragraph openings. You can link ideas with useful discourse markers, such as:

  Firstly...
  Secondly...
  What is more...
  On the other hand...
  In addition...

  and so on.
- You might introduce a situation and use it to prove your point:

  ... This shows, only too clearly, that...
- Alternatively, you might make various claims, then move to an incident which illustrates what you are saying:

  There is certainly no doubt things could be better. Only last week when my mother...
- You should use a definite conclusion, which promotes one point of view and leaves the reader believing you must be right:

  Young people, therefore, are not hooligans. They do not set out to make others' lives a misery and they do care about the world. They are simply tarred with the same brush as the small minority who can cause problems and are defamed by the media at every opportunity.

Writing to argue (1–2)

1 Place the following ideas into a logical order: (6)

A Therefore, the odds against winning are enormous.
B Most players have more than one go.
C 8 million people buy lottery tickets regularly.
D They are almost too large to be calculated.
E Some say only a fool would get involved in this gamble.
F Only two or three people win the jackpot each week.

2 Read the following extract from a newspaper article, and select the discourse markers which most logically fill the gaps.

This country loves its football. Increasingly, even women follow the sport. **A** ________ , (1) football stadia can be very unpleasant places and football is still not family-orientated. Who would want, **B** ________ , (1) to be a Spurs fan in the middle of the Arsenal section of the ground? **C** ________ , (1) would you want your young children to hear the language fired at most referees during most games? **D** ________ , (1) football needs to make improvements to become part of the twenty-first century.

Choose from:

for example	come what may	on the other hand	similarly
later	coincidentally	in other words	however

3 Join statements from the two columns to make logical pairs. (10)

1 Holidays in Europe broaden the mind.
2 Top politicians sometimes join the European Commission.
3 People are really similar, wherever they live.
4 Britain can learn much from its neighbours.
5 Not all Britons are small-minded.

A The ex-leader of the Labour Party is a perfect example.
B For a start, we do not have to be obsessed by work.
C We can get a different perspective on world affairs.
D There is more to us than a love of fish and chips.
E The desire for a better life style is a common goal.

SCORE

1 **C**, **B**, **F**, **A**, **D**, **E** (6)

There can be some flexibility in what is acceptable here. The statement 'Some say only a fool would get involved in this gamble', for example, might come immediately after **B**. The important point, though, is that each idea must follow logically from what has gone before it. If you 'lose' your reader, you cannot be convincing.

2 **A** = however (1)
B = for example (1)
C = similarly (1)
D = in other words (*or* come what may) (1)

Discourse markers are the simplest way to link ideas effectively. Most can be used in any argue, persuade, advise response. It is sometimes worth jotting down a list of them before you begin to write, so that you can dip in and choose an appropriate one when it is needed. Another priority, since you will use these expressions so regularly, is to make sure you can spell them all correctly.

3 **1 C**; (2) **2 A**; (2) **3 E**; (2) **4 B**; (2) **5 D** (2)

We are dealing here with a simple linking of ideas, but sections of a response must be joined in much the same way. When one thought does not flow logically from another, we call it a non sequitur, and these are best avoided.

TOTAL

Opposing viewpoints

When you are writing, you must show that you understand the point of view you are arguing against: there must be at least two sides to an argument. You might choose to:

- set out one point of view

then

- argue against it

or, you can:

- set out one powerful argument, concentrating on that side

but

- make references which show you are aware of another viewpoint ('Of course, some argue that shopping is perfect relaxation. However, for many people, this is not the case. Consider the example of...')

or, you can

- make a point, then argue against it
- make another point and argue against that

and so on.

High-quality features

Simply telling someone what you think can prove extremely boring for your audience. Whenever you produce a response for Section B, if you interest the reader, you are likely to be awarded higher marks. The more entertaining your response, the more convincing you will seem. You should include features to bring your writing to life and allow the examiner to reward you, such as:

Anecdote

Comedians usually base part of their act on short stories: 'real life' instances that illustrate the point they are making. Your task in the examination is not to produce a comedy routine, but you can use the same technique. An anecdote, showing *how* someone has been affected, for example, is usually more effective than making a bare statement.

I think old people should be treated better. ✗
Old people require more care. Only yesterday, newspapers reported the story of an old man who died in his flat and was not discovered for over a week... ✓

Rhetorical language

When language is used for a particular effect, we call it rhetorical. The simplest way to employ rhetoric in your response is to use rhetorical questions to help argue your case. These are questions which make a point by challenging the reader, but only expecting the answer you yourself would give:

> Surely this confusion needs sorting out? (Logical answer: 'Yes, it does!')
> How can anyone doubt they are doing this for the best possible motives? (Logical answer: 'No one can!')
> Should we just stand by and let it happen? (Logical answer: 'Certainly not!')

Examples

Without some form of apparent proof, your argument might not be convincing. Examples which prove your points, therefore, are essential. These might come in the form of anecdotes; or statistics, which you might have to invent in the examination ('Recent research has found that 93% of school leavers would never consider teaching as a career'); or other factual references ('Princess Diana suffered exactly this fate.').

Quotations

Again, you might have to make up supportive quotations in an examination, but they can give your argument considerable weight, if used sparingly and appropriately:

> 'As the Prime Minister said in parliament, "…"'
> 'My own grandmother, who had lived through both world wars, used to say, "…"'

Humour

It is unlikely you will need to tell jokes in your response, but using exaggeration, sarcasm or unexpected detail can bring light relief to an argument and will be rewarded by the examiner. If someone is laughing with you, they are more likely to be on your side. You should not go overboard in your attempt to raise a smile, but you can include humorous touches:

> My eyes were popping out. And doing somersaults... [Exaggeration]
> Only someone with no nose could live with the smell… [Sarcasm]
> Our headteacher kept us terrified. Until, one day, his false teeth fell out in assembly… [Unexpected]

Writing to argue (3–4)

1 Which high-quality features have been used by this GCSE candidate, whilst arguing that school holidays should be spread more evenly across the year? (6)

2 How has the argument been structured? (14)

Anyone looking with fresh eyes at the way our holidays are organised can see that the present pattern is silly. Terms vary in length, teaching and learning are disrupted and although students look forward to the summer break, for many it becomes a period of boredom and frustration.

Of course, some will argue that what we have is what we are used to; that change will disrupt families' routines; and that to have, for example, eight half terms of roughly equal length, with the same amount of holiday after each one, would make for monotony and would give students little to look forward to. Yet, some people have no imagination to begin with.

'School terms dragged like a heavy sack,' wrote Richard Evans in his autobiography, and he was right, at least in part. Worst of all is the autumn term, where students toil with heavy hearts, living for Christmas to end the misery. Can you learn properly when the brain is addled and the spirit jaded? No one can, and no one does. When a friend of mine fell asleep in History, no one seemed surprised, least of all the teacher, who suggested we all bring sleeping bags the next day.

Instead of such tedium, we need shorter, sharper periods of teaching and more regular and healthy breaks. It could work. Education authorities which have taken steps to trial new holiday patterns report positive feedback from students and teachers alike. That can only lead to improved results.

Imagine a world where schools could look forward to a break every four, five or six weeks and could still enjoy a month's break in the heat of summer. How could anyone say that wouldn't be better for all?

SCORE

1 sarcasm ('some people have no imagination to begin with'); (1) rhetorical questions ('Can you learn properly...?' and 'How Could anyone say...?'); (2) quotation (from Richard Evans); (1) anecdote ('When a friend of mine...'); (1) example ('Education authorities...') (1)

Reading and writing skills need to be inter-changeable. In other words, having seen how this candidate has constructed her argument, try to use these features in your own work.

It is worth noting that the candidate was also using other obvious techniques to enrich her writing: lists to build effect (such as in the second sentence), emotive language ('toil with heavy hearts'; 'the spirit jaded') and a variety of sentence lengths – notice the long sentence in the second paragraph, juxtaposed with the brief, sarcastic reply at the end of that paragraph. Later, there is the powerful simplicity of 'It could work.'

2 The response begins with a clear statement of the writer's feelings. (2) The second paragraph presents an opposite viewpoint, (2) but immediately seeks to undermine it. (2) The third paragraph, the longest, uses a range of techniques to hammer home the writer's feelings; (2) and the fourth moves to stress the benefits of change. (2) The text ends with a vision of an improved future and a rhetorical plea to the reader which seems difficult to argue against. (2) Discourse markers are employed to link ideas, when necessary ('Of course... Yet...'). (2)

In an examination, you might produce a longer response, but could reproduce the sort of effects created here. Notice that the writer knew exactly what she intended to say from the very first line and that her ideas were never jumbled. We imagine that a careful plan preceded this actual response.

TOTAL

WRITING TO PERSUADE (1)

To **persuade**, you must convince the reader to agree with you. Sometimes, you might persuade by using logical argument; or, you can present just **one point of view**. For instance, see how the NatWest Bank tries to win new customers:

> **NatWest**
> More than just a bank
>
> Everyone needs to escape sometimes, and with a NatWest credit card, the world's your oyster. It's accepted at over 14 million outlets worldwide, which makes it the ideal getaway card. For details, call 0800 616 848 or pop into your local branch.

It is 'selling' its credit card by saying it offers 'escape'. This is to make the reader think the card will give them freedom, a breath of fresh air. Also, if the world becomes 'your oyster', that cliché implies pearls and wealth, so the card is definitely worth having. In addition, it can be used across the globe ('14 million outlets worldwide'), so the implication is that having the card introduces you to travel, or makes travelling that much easier. Indeed, it is described as the 'ideal getaway card', so, presumably, users can get away from their mundane existence. Not only that, it seems easy to acquire: 'pop into your local branch'. 'Pop' suggests it will only take a moment – and might even be fun.

This is how one newspaper wrote about personality Chris Evans:

> **Where did it all go wrong? Commentators say the £50million presenter-cum-producer has fallen out of touch.**
>
> 'I don't think his career is all over but he certainly seems out of sorts,' said GQ editor Dylan Jones. 'It's no longer the mid-90s and people are more interested in Big Brother... For the time being at least, Chris Evans is so 20th century.'
>
> *Metro News*

If you use a question, you can suggest a way of thinking (things have gone wrong...); experts can support your claim ('commentators'); and they can present your ideas (Chris Evans appears out of date and – temporarily at least – out of fashion).

At times, persuasive writing '**browbeats**' the reader, as the editor does in this column from *The Observer*:

> Sport must no longer be an add-on, squeezed into the national curriculum as an afterthought. Tony Blair, who takes pride in his own physical fitness, must make some radical changes to both the school day and its curriculum. If that means less time for endless testing, children may find they are winners twice over.

Like this writer, you can use repetition to convince the reader. If your tone of voice is definite, you allow no doubt to cloud the issue. Then, a final clinching point can be most effective ('they are the winners twice over').

Newspaper writing will usually be formal. However, persuasive writing can sometimes be **less formal**, because in some circumstances the reader will find that style to be more appropriate, for example:

- in a letter persuading a friend, relative or colleague
- in an autobiographical account
- in texts where the writer sets out very personal opinions.

Notice the **mood** of this extract, in which Mike Harding writes about computers:

> But you can't carry a computer on the bus and read it standing up, you can't sit in the khazi with a computer on your knee reading it while the foreman wonders where you are, you can't wrap chips or flatten flies with a computer, and you can't cut a computer up into squares, put a string through it and hang it on the back of the thunderbox door. You can't even amuse the kids by bending it and tearing it and turning it into a tree or a line of clowns.
>
> *Hypnotising the Cat*

To persuade you, he uses abbreviations ('can't') and humour (the idea of using newspaper as toilet paper and calling the toilet the 'thunderbox').

Writing to Persuade (3)

Consider this essay title:

> Write an article for a national newspaper, to persuade the readers to campaign for improvements in our transport systems.

If faced with such a task, you would:

- decide whether to deal with all the different modes of transport, or concentrate on just one or two (e.g. road and rail)
- plan your response with an interesting introduction, logical progression and convincing conclusion
- concentrate on an appropriate style: in this case, it would almost certainly be formal.

You would also have to decide which techniques might be most effective, to support your case. Although you could use them at any stage in your response, you might adopt the following approach:

Opening

You could capture the reader's sympathies with the use of **emotive language**, designed to touch their emotions so that they engage sympathetically with your ideas:

> Picture the scene: it is a windswept platform, somewhere in Derbyshire, and the rain is sweeping in from the west. Commuters stand in the open, desperately peering up the line in the hope that their train will come. Skirts and trousers are soaking and faces are grim. The transport system is failing once again...

You would be hoping anyone who had been in such a situation would sympathise; and those who had not could imagine the discomfort.

You might then move into the main body of your article following a challenging and **rhetorical question**, designed to further gain readers' support:

> Isn't it time the country invested in transport systems and moved into the twenty-first century?

Main body of essay

Varying your techniques is a good way of engaging the reader's interest – and gaining higher marks. So, as well as using **quotation**, to add weight to your ideas:

> Lord Emmanuel, who headed an independent inquiry into commuter problems, declared: 'Investment is the only solution...'

you can use **repetition** or a **list** to hammer home a message:

> The situation seems dire. The roads are jammed; the railways are running late; air traffic controllers are stretched to breaking point; and the canals are considered too slow to be of any help.

Notice too, how a variety of sentences can be effective. The first sentence, ending with 'dire', is punchy and, apparently, unanswerable; the long sentence which follows adds detail to the claim.

If you also choose to use **exaggeration for effect**, you might wish to blend that with light **humour**, since it is easier to persuade people if you can also make them smile:

> I just wish I could tell my eighty-five year old grandmother that she no longer needs her skateboard, because there are going to be buses running through her estate again. Yet, unless government acts, she will need a new helmet next Christmas. Again.

Ending

You need to:

- sum up your viewpoint

and, if possible,

- make a final, decisive point.

You might, for instance, make use of **figurative language**, in which imagery clarifies a point or brings it to life:

> Like an exhausted marathon runner, the transport system is grinding to a halt. It needs more than a massage. Without a new coach and a truly professional approach, it will never be successful...

Writing to persuade (1–4)

1 Below is the first paragraph of an article by George Adamson in the TES, persuading readers that schools should concentrate on teaching, not grading.

> My daughter is nine years old, so you can imagine how disheartened I was to read a file, written by her on my laptop, which included the words 'When I get older, I don't want to go to university because I am not very clever now.'

Explain why you might choose each of the following sentences to continue the article.

A Had the school shattered her confidence for ever? (3)

B She was depressed and demoralised and her hopes had been destroyed. (3)

C It felt like a spark had died in her soul. (3)

D The hopelessness of her words is with me every waking moment. (3)

2 Later in the article comes this extract:

> For my daughter, being put in a low set for English and Maths was enough to give this message about her perceived lack of intelligence. The upward spiral is great if it works that way, but for many the downward spiral can move dangerously fast and become difficult – and perhaps impossible – to stop.
>
> Where this spiral ends is anyone's guess: the murky depths of depression, a painful anxiety-filled existence? Who knows?

Write a paragraph to persuade readers to the opposite point of view: that being put in a lower set can be helpful. (8)

Make sure you use:

- a rhetorical question
- some emotive language
- a statement from someone supporting your ideas (you can make it up if you wish)
- repetition for effect.

SCORE

1 **A** A rhetorical question is likely to make the reader agree that her confidence has been shattered; (1) the figurative language ('shattered her confidence') makes the point vividly; (1) and the damage is made to seem huge ('for ever'). (1)

B Three statements are made to hammer home the damage; (1) alliteration makes them more memorable; (1) and all three significant words (depressed/demoralised/destroyed) suggest misery. (1)

C Imagery is used to bring the point to life ('spark had died'); (1) the point seems exaggerated; (1) and the anguish has an almost spiritual side to it ('soul'). (1)

D Again there is exaggeration ('every waking moment'); (1) there is the greatest stress on 'hopelessness' to begin the sentence; (1) and we are persuaded to feel sympathy for both the child and the parent ('is with me'). (1)

When you are writing persuasively, you will be creating effects, not analysing them in this way. Nevertheless, if you select language effectively, you can influence the reader in similar ways. It is helpful, therefore, to read other texts analytically, as part of a revision programme, then aim to mirror the techniques in your own work.

2 In your paragraph, you should have included:

- a rhetorical question to further your persuasion (such as: 'Don't children need to be tested so teachers know their weaknesses?' or 'Surely this is best?') (2)
- emotive language – perhaps stressing how setting can improve performance (e.g. 'The weakest can grow and develop and lose their fears.') (2)
- a convincing statement of support (e.g. 'One leading headteacher said…') (2)
- repetition – perhaps using three points together (e.g. 'In suitable sets, children receive care, guidance and work that is appropriate…'). (2)

The art of persuasion does not lie in following a formula, and the fact that you have used these techniques cannot guarantee examination success. That depends on many factors, including how well you can use these approaches in the structure of your response. Nevertheless, having them at your fingertips is an excellent starting point.

TOTAL

Writing to advise (1)

As with any other form of writing, you will find it easier to write to advise if you have read widely, and noticed what professional writers produce. Newspapers and magazines are a ready source of advice – offered on a range of subjects: to politicians, to girls who have lost their boyfriends, and so on. However, such advice will have common features. It will be:

- clear – the reader must know exactly what you are suggesting;
- logical – if your advice does not make sense, it will not be accepted;
- definite – you will almost certainly need to use the imperative voice, telling the reader what is needed: 'Seize the moment...'; 'Don't delay...'; 'Wake up and respond now, before it is too late...'.

When writing to advise, you will need to **convince or persuade** the reader, and might, possibly, use **argument**, to make the advice seem sensible. You can, therefore, use the skills dealt with in the two previous units. In particular, ideas must link smoothly and lead to a logical conclusion. One difference, though, is that when advising you will also be telling the reader what to do, so it is vital that you sound knowledgeable and confident.

If the advice is to be accepted, ensure you are always responding appropriately to the given **purpose and audience**. Some advice might be very formal, for instance, if you write a letter to the local council, to advise its members how they should spend a recently acquired lottery grant: 'If you look at the situation logically, the best ways to spend the money are clear...' Other advice could be less formal, such as when you write a letter to an elderly and distant relative, advising her about how to protect her bungalow against burglars: 'Trust me, auntie – replacing your old alarm system's an A1 idea...'

Your advice will usually benefit from:

- examples
- anecdotes
- supportive quotations
- humour, when appropriate.

Writing to advise (2)

Here are the final paragraphs from two GCSE candidates who were asked to advise a holiday firm how to improve its package holidays.

Candidate 1

I think you might be able to do better. The coaches you use are a bit old and some people might think they aren't comfortable. I think they are OK but some people might not agree. So you could change them if you wanted and that might mean you could become more popular and make more money.

Notice here:

- 'might' is used four times: the advice, therefore, does not sound definite;
- the advice is undermined when the writer says: 'I think they are OK';
- the conditional tense ('You could change them…') is unlikely to provoke instant action; it does not give the impression the writer feels this course of action is vital.

Candidate 2

Above all, the company must redesign its image. It has to look like a firm which is facing the future with confidence, so that customers will have faith in it. You need to commission a new advertising campaign, offer better deals for families, train your staff better in customer relations and check that your hotels, coaches and planes are clean, and run efficiently. That will guarantee you will have no further problems. You can then head towards the brightest of futures.

In this case:

- the tone is definite: 'must', 'has to';
- the imperative verbs allow no opportunity for doubt: 'find', 'offer', 'train', 'check';
- the listing of ideas seems to make the case irresistible;
- the penultimate sentence promises success: 'That will guarantee…';
- there is a clear sense here of a thorough case being summed up and re-stated briefly for effect, and finished off with an appropriately positive final sentence.

Writing to advise (1–2)

1 These are the opening sentences from four paragraphs of a text offering advice. Put them into a logical order: (4)

A Consider the alternatives and the difficulties they will bring...
B If you follow this advice...
C Your problems fall into two categories...
D The solution, then, must be to...

2 Match each of the following sentences with one of the given purposes and audiences. Say, in each case, what makes them suitable: (12)

A Just get on and do it.	**(i)** Letter from head-teacher to students
B Strive harder and I have no doubt you will succeed.	**(ii)** Government circular to business leaders
C You really should think about the effect this might have on others.	**(iii)** Letter to a friend
D Organisations wishing to take advantage of this offer must endeavour to...	**(iv)** 'Agony aunt' column in women's magazine

3 If you were writing to advise, which of these alternatives might you use, and why? (4)

A You **must/should/could** invest in some new clothes.
B The result **would/might** be impressive.

ANSWERS & TUTORIALS

SCORE

1 Most suitable sequence: C, A, D, B. (4)
Although there can be no perfect pattern for all responses, the organisation here is a reliable template for other situations. Ideally, there would be an introduction, then:

1. the problems are defined
2. approaches/solutions are presented
3. alternatives are dealt with
4. a firm conclusion is presented.

2 **A** (iii); (1) conversational tone ('Get on'); (1) monosyllabic words – with just one syllable – produce a direct approach likely to be effective with a friend. (1)

B (i); (1) sense of someone who knows all the answers; (1) vocabulary appropriate for world of education ('strive'/ 'succeed'). (1)

C (iv); (1) lighter touch, trying to 'win round' the reader; (1) persuading her to accept the advice through sounding very reasonable and balanced. (1)

D (ii); (1) voice of authority ('must'); (1) and aimed at an educated audience ('endeavour') (1) (or, alternatively, clearly the beginning of a complex sentence).

3 Any alternative acceptable, so long as the explanation is suitable:

A 'must': definite, allows no contradiction – the advice is really an instruction; 'should': confident and sounds persuasive; 'could': in some instances, might seem lacking in conviction – but could be offering a solution, believing the reader will accept this course of action. (2)

B 'would': result clear, no doubt about outcome; 'might': in some instances, might seem lacking in conviction – but could be suggesting the outcome might bring a pleasant outcome, in the right context. (2)

'Could' and 'might' are generally best avoided, but can be effective if used appropriately and provided they do not contribute to an overall effect of vagueness. Again, it is worth seeing how professionals use such vocabulary: reading is usually the key to improved writing.

TOTAL

WRITING TO INFORM, EXPLAIN, DESCRIBE (1)

When writing to:

- **inform** – you give details, facts, information
- **explain** – you present the reasons why or how things happen
- **describe** – you present a picture for the reader.

In each case, the response should be **structured**. Avoid simply listing relevant details or setting down jumbled thoughts. Show an understanding of how such writing is tailored to be effective. A plan is essential.

Possible question: Explain what makes your school special.

Possible plan:

1 Introduction: name and type of school/general factual information
2 Reason 1: ... (detail)
3 Reason 2: ... (linked from first reason – detail)
4 Reason 3: ... (linked from second reason – detail)
5 Conclusion: summing up the school's positive features

Writing to inform

To be awarded a good grade, informative writing must be specific. For example:
General: 'Travel agents offer you holidays all over the world.'
Specific: 'Travel agents offer a wide variety of holidays, in a huge range of locations: from skiing in Austria, to baking in the Bahamas; from...'

Writing to explain

An explanation goes behind the information to say 'why' or 'how':

Simple response (Grade F/G):

I spend my time swimming because I love being in the water.

Higher level response (Grade C+):

Because I have always enjoyed acting, I spend most of my free time at a drama club. This allows me to develop my abilities in various ways. For instance...

Here, the subject is explained at some length and the candidate is already filling in details, so that we do not need to guess.

Writing to inform, explain, describe (2)

Possible question:

Write an article informing readers of a travel magazine about your favourite holiday destination, and explaining its attraction.

Possible openings:

1

Like most people, I enjoy holidays abroad. For me, nowhere could be better than Fuerteventura in the Canary Islands, which has so many attractions. I love being there.

The destination is clearly identified, the purpose is addressed and the attractions might be discussed next.

2

Fuerteventura is the perfect place for an escape from Britain, at any time of the year. It has the cute wildlife of Chipmonk Mountain, the beach at Corralejo and lagoons in the south.

Having begun with a list, the candidate will need to go on to write about those significant features in detail, explaining the attraction of each.

Middle section:

We go to Fuerteventura every Easter, and stay for a week at Caleta de Fuste. All day we sit on a beach, windsurf or travel round in a rented jeep; at night there are restaurants, bars and karaoke competitions, so my dad is in his element and we are in hysterics.

This extract shows the candidate is still 'on track'. There is information, explanation (why they enjoy the island) and humour at the end.

Ending:

I cannot recommend Fuerteventura too highly. It offers everything you could expect of a sun-drenched island, and gives my family something to look forward to for twelve whole months. I just hope it never changes.

Personal response

Summarises information

Summarises explanation

Effective summative comment

Writing to inform, explain, describe (1–2)

1 Choose 3 of the following sentences, each of which could begin an informative response. What might the remainder of those 3 texts contain? (6)

A Despite significant changes in recent years, the royal family is still in a very privileged position.

B Without qualifications, it is difficult to be successful in the jobs market.

C My interest in fashion is as strong as ever.

D Should we trust the government?

E From the first time I saw him, I knew he was the only one for me.

2 Complete these sentences by adding an explanation. Use a different conjunction each time, to link what you write to the words given. (8)

(a) Modern cars are safer...

(b) Mobile phones have transformed people's lives...

(c) Global warming seems to be accelerating and is becoming an alarming phenomenon...

(d) Growing older can be a pleasure...

3 (a) Write a paragraph containing three pieces of information about the place where you live, and designed to interest a visitor. Number each detail. (3)

(b) Write one paragraph about each piece of information, explaining in detail why it might be of interest. (3)

SCORE

1 (Only 3 of these totalling 6 marks)

A Facts and information about the royals (perhaps 'then and now'); an attempt to contrast them with the rest of the population. (2)

B (A*ny two of*) Possibly the range of jobs requiring qualifications; which jobs need/do not need qualifications; possibly some focus on particular jobs' requirements. (2)

C Information about why there is this interest in fashion; perhaps detail on what this interest has provoked and/or where it might lead. (2)

D This seems more an argue/persuade opening, but could inform about government approaches: what people think about them; what they have done and intend to do. (2)

E Details about the meeting; and what makes him attractive. (2)

This is an instance in which many other details could be offered, and provided they supply information, you can award them marks. The important point is to attempt to offer detail, develop ideas and to avoid straying into lengthy explanation if information is required.

2 Conjunctions are likely to be words like 'because', 'since', 'by', 'through', 'as', etc. Award 1 mark for each conjunction used appropriately and not used previously, and 1 mark for each sensible explanation. (8)

Here you are employing conjunctions, but it is always worth trying to vary the vocabulary used. Repeated phrasing results in lower marks.

3 **(a)** There should be three distinct pieces of information. (3)

(b) Paragraphs should be sufficiently detailed – for example, moving beyond 'because it's an exciting place to be', or equivalent. An explanation might, for instance, say: 'The castle has a history which dates back to… Many of the original walls are still standing, and… Some visitors have even said that…' (3) (1 mark for each detailed paragraph)

Although this task simply requires three paragraphs, and there are no other instructions, remember that a structured response should include links between ideas, and would normally include discourse markers like 'furthermore', 'in addition', 'meanwhile, at the other end of town…' and so on.

TOTAL

Writing to describe

Descriptive writing should avoid narrative. The examiner is not interested in story. It is most likely you will be asked to describe a person or place, atmosphere or situation.

Throughout, the description should be concentrated and related to purpose. This description of Cittagazze is taken from *The Subtle Knife* by Philip Pullman:

> The air of the place had something Mediterranean or maybe Caribbean about it. Will had never been out of England, so he couldn't compare it with anywhere he knew, but it was the kind of place where people came out late at night to eat and drink, to dance and enjoy music. Except that there was no one here, and the silence was immense.
>
> On the first corner he reached there stood a café, with little green tables on the pavement and a zinc-topped bar and an expresso machine. On some of the tables glasses stood half-empty; in an ashtray a cigarette had burned down to the butt; a plate of risotto stood next to a basket of stale rolls as hard as cardboard...

Notice how he:

- focuses on atmosphere ('the silence was immense')
- implies mystery, as if everyone fled suddenly a while ago ('glasses stood half-empty .... stale rolls as hard as cardboard')
- uses precise detail to present the scene.

Your own response should be planned and structured so it draws to a memorable conclusion, perhaps:

- adding one final detail:

  'And, as the lights go out, only the old man under the pier remains on the beach, wrapped in rags against the wind.'
- or summing up what has been said:

  'That's just what my mother is like: kind, loving, determined, fierce, loyal, trusting and, beneath it all, quite insecure. It's a strange mix, and so is she.'
- or challenging the reader:

  'Could any town be more perfect? Could anywhere be more peaceful? Surely, such a place would be hard to find.'

WRITING TO INFORM, EXPLAIN, DESCRIBE (4)

There is a range of strategies which can help you improve the quality of your descriptions.

- Use of the five senses (hearing, taste, touch, sight and smell):

> The wallpaper looks a century old, and the walls are cold to touch. The house is very old and smells of mould in the whitewashed kitchen. The food served by Aunt Grace always seems to have a hint of peppermint, and her voice creaks, like a gate in a windy yard.

- The use of similes and metaphors, which can add originality if clichés are avoided (for example, 'a nose like a ski slope'):

> Aunty's guest room is like a cave [simile] and is filled with the ghosts of travellers who have lodged there over the years [metaphor]. If you lie there at night, as still as a tombstone [simile], the past envelops you [metaphor].

- The selective use of speech can bring a scene to life, but should only be used for illustrative purposes, to make a brief point:

> My aunt is like a living part of the cottage. 'I feel as if I've been here since time began,' she laughs, rocking in her chair, and you believe her.

- Anecdotes – if brief – can add further life and add to the impression you are creating:

> Once, a gasman who had called ran from the cellar, screaming. He said there were strange noises down there and fled, leaving the meter unread. Aunt Grace said it had just been her stomach rumbling, but was delighted at the thought of not getting a bill!

Writing to inform, explain, describe (3–4)

1 **(a)** Write briefly what might be included in five sections of a response describing autumn. (5)

(b) Write the first topic sentence for each of your paragraphs, ensuring there is a link with what has gone before. (5)

2 Continue this description of a park on a quiet afternoon. Include at least 3 similes and 3 metaphors: (6)

> There was a stillness lying across the grass. No breeze shifted the branches of the trees, which were heavy with greenness. No ripples ran across the lake. A few voices could be heard, echoing in the distance, but there was a heaviness that made everything slow, muffled and hot.

3 Read the following description and then decide where you could add 2 brief quotations to contribute to its effect: (4)

> He was tall and sombre. If ever he spoke, his words were slow, and seemed measured. Some believed that because he had lived in America, he saw himself as some sort of cowboy; others, less sympathetic, said he wasn't very bright and his brain took an age to come up with any idea.

SCORE

1 **(a)** 1 mark for each section, each of which should relate directly to autumn, for example:

i weather begins to change colours in gardens and parks (1)

ii hibernation of animals (1)

iii effect in houses (1)

iv effect on people's habits (1)

v winter approaching (1)

(b) 1 mark for each appropriate topic sentence. All but the first should link with what would have appeared in the previous paragraph, for example:

iii *Inside houses, too, there are changes, as the central heating is tested and windows are more often closed...* (5)

2 1 mark for each appropriate simile or metaphor – the similes should be introduced by 'like' or 'as' and the metaphors should state things which are not literally true. In each case, the image must be appropriate for the purpose, i.e. it must develop the description of the park and contribute to the given atmosphere. For example:

The ice cream van, when it arrived, was the children's salvation. (6)

Be aware of the fact that descriptions which rely too heavily on similes and metaphors can seem 'overdone'; also, it is difficult to produce streams of original and effective images. However, their selective inclusion will certainly improve the mark awarded.

3 Ideally, the quotations should be no more than 10–12 words long. One could be used, for example, after the second sentence:

...slow and measured: 'There must be a good reason.'

or, after

...saw himself as some sort of cowboy: 'The West must have been a fine place to be.'

or, could even come in the middle of a sentence:

...because he had lived in America ('I was a trail hand at the age of eight'), *he saw himself...*

2 marks for each suitable quotation, which must prove the point made immediately before it, in the text. (4)

TOTAL

WRITING TO ANALYSE, REVIEW, COMMENT (1)

These three forms of writing are very closely related. An **analysis** requires a precise examination of some topic; that examination is likely to constitute a **review**; and, in analysing or reviewing, a writer will almost certainly **comment** on the subject matter.

Look at this review of a new approach to eating on the move:

> *Backpacker* (August) introduced its readers to edible gear. That's right, a rucksack you can eat. 'No doubt you've heard the legends of desperate adventurers eking a few calories of sustenance out of boot leather,' said the magazine. 'The founders of Eastern Active Technologies (Eat) think those poor souls were on to something. Eat has developed a full line of backpacking equipment made from sugar, carb and meat-based materials... Sounds crazy, but consider the potential weight savings: you can leave the usual foodstuffs at home, but every meal makes you lighter.'
>
> The magazine put a Snack-Pack to the test on a four-day trek in Montana's Bitterroot Mountains. They found the 'mango-flavoured material was pleasantly chewy and packed with energy (350 calories and 25 grams of carbohydrate per square inch)'. However, you should plan meals wisely, otherwise 'you risk serious discomfort in the final miles (one tester munched his hipbelt prematurely and paid for it)'.
>
> *The Guardian*

The review, as well as giving a general impression of the edible rucksack, begins to analyse some elements (its attractive flavour and nutritional value) and comments on the item: 'Sounds crazy'/'However, you should plan your meals wisely...'

It is also worth noting here how precise the detail is. The writer also endeavours to entertain the reader with humour – for example, in the final sentence. A candidate who can analyse with tongue-in-cheek will be rewarded by the examiner who will appreciate the originality and welcome any appropriate use of irony or exaggeration.

WRITING TO ANALYSE, REVIEW, COMMENT (2)

Detail is essential when reviewing and analysing.

These two extracts come from candidates who were asked to review their five years in high school:

Candidate 1

> Lots of things are wrong with the school, but it's not all bad. Some people quite enjoyed their five years but others didn't. There were things that should have been better in the lessons and even the rules should have been changed. I'm glad I'm escaping at last.

This response:

- is full of generalisations ('lots of things', 'there were things');
- contains criticisms which might be valid but are not proven;
- has no developments, so ideas are jumbled together (lessons and rules, for example).

The final comment is vivid, but would have been more convincing if it had followed detailed analysis.

Candidate 2

> Most of the school rules, I see now, have a purpose. For example, I used to be annoyed by our one-way system, but it certainly makes movement around the buildings easier and safer; and I couldn't understand why we were forced to wear school uniform, but it certainly saved my parents money.
>
> Of course, some rules were petty and unnecessary. Take, for instance, the rule that...

In this case:

- there are sensible paragraphs, with topic sentences;
- discourse markers usefully link ideas ('For example', 'Of course');
- detail supports the views throughout (though, as ever, there could have been more, e.g. description of the uniform, focusing on those items which cause most dispute).

Overall, Candidate 2 is more convincing because we understand why she feels as she does.

Writing to analyse, review, comment (1–2)

1 Plan a review of a television programme of your choice. (20)

- Make sure the plan is detailed.
- Show why you like or dislike it.
- Examine different features of the programme, including scheduling, individuals who are involved, sets, the nature of the drama or the way the programme is put together, humour, audience reaction, and so on.
- Compare it with other programmes, if you wish.

Set out your plan appropriately. You might wish to use this layout:

Paragraph	Central idea in the paragraph	Details to be included
1		1… 2… 3… etc.
2		1… 2… 3… etc.
3		

SCORE

1 Mark your plan using the following descriptors.

Like an examiner, use a best-fit principle. So, for example, if all the 6–10 descriptors apply to your work, you get 10 marks; however, if there is no logical structure, so that ideas do not follow in a sensible order, but there are 2 or 3 precise details in each section, award 8, and so on. (20)

Marks	Content descriptors
1–5	● Some ideas ● Only one or two details in each section ● Details likely to be very briefly presented (probably just one or two words)
6–10	● Ideas beginning to be structured so ideas follow with some logic ● At least two or three details in each section ● Details better explained
11–15	● Structured plan, with ideas following logically ● At least three precise, explained details in each section ● Possibly details of what might be in an introduction and conclusion
16–20	● A full plan, with an introduction and conclusion ● Each section has three, four or more points ● Detailed throughout and clearly explained

Careful planning is one key to successful writing in the examination. Structure and paragraphing are both awarded marks, and these are areas overlooked by many candidates. However, there is no point in producing a plan unless it is intended to inform the writing process, so the more detail you give, the better. Those candidates who produce a plan and then totally ignore it when they begin to write the response have simply wasted their time, of course.

TOTAL

WRITING TO ANALYSE, REVIEW, COMMENT (3)

When you make comments, they need to be relevant and, wherever possible, should arise from what you have revealed in your analysis. So, for instance, while it is valid to write 'Modern music is getting better all the time', such a comment would carry more weight if it grew from, or was followed by, a review of certain releases or artists, which compared them favourably with music that has been produced in the past.

The following extract is part of a 'comment' column from the *Daily Mail*. Notice how the initial comment is immediately supported by relevant detail:

Into the bottomless pit of Britain's transport shambles pours an ever-increasing cascade of public money. According to the Royal Geographical Society, railway subsidies are £250million a year higher than in the nationalised days of British Rail. The cost to the taxpayer now exceeds £1.3billion annually…

In this letter from *The Times*, the comment is in different forms. There is an initial, **straightforward comment** with which many would agree; and a more subtle ending, which grows out of the body of the letter and merely **suggests** that the old ways were better:

Sir, Bullying is the worst thing that can happen in school.

Unfortunately, it seems very much more common than I remember when I was at primary school and grammar school in the 1930s and 1940s. I can recall only one instance and that was at my grammar school. The culprit came to the notice of the headmaster. He received three of the best on his backside and never bullied again. As far as I know he went on to have a successful career in the Civil Service.

I wonder whether the behavioural consultants proposed by the government will be as successful.

WRITING TO ANALYSE, REVIEW, COMMENT (4)

Let's consider how to deal with this question:

> Write a review of an event you have attended.
>
> You might wish to:
> - analyse its success or/and its failings
> - comment on how it could be improved.

In this case, the title allows you to select a relatively major event (e.g. cup final, school speech day); or a more personal event with significance for you (e.g. a family day out, birthday celebration). Also, you can praise it, criticise, or balance your views, but are encouraged to say what might have made it better. It is always necessary to know what your opinion is **before** you begin to write: a change of viewpoint always stands out and will reduce your marks.

A possible approach

1 Introduction

Details of the event – when and where – who attended – general comments on it, to be expanded in the body of the response.

2 What happened and how successful it was

Event dealt with:

- chronologically – what happened in what order

or

- examining particular elements of the event, in turn.

3 Conclusion

Summary of the event, drawing to a clear final opinion which emerges logically from what has gone before.

Comment could be made at regular intervals, or at the end of each paragraph or section. In either case, it is more convincing if the comment supports the impression given in the opening paragraph and re-stated in the conclusion.

Avoid muddled thinking. If you are aware of good and bad features, put them in two defined sections: don't jumble them together.

Writing to analyse, review, comment (3–4)

1 Write a full answer to the following question.

> **It is often said that young people are selfish and don't care enough about the world.**
>
> **Comment on how true you find this point of view, and analyse the attitudes of young people you know.** (20)

You might wish to:

- focus on just two or three people you know or on a larger group;
- write about attitudes to environmental or social issues;
- make straightforward comments and/or more subtle ones which are implied, or, perhaps, come from challenges to the reader (e.g. 'Can anyone honestly believe that...?').

Remember to:

- plan your response carefully and structure your ideas;
- write 1–1½ pages of A4;
- vary the length of your sentences and paragraphs;
- use appropriate vocabulary and avoid repetition;
- punctuate accurately and demonstrate the range of your ability (if you can use colons and semi-colons, for example, show the examiner);
- take care with spellings;
- try to use an anecdote, examples, quotations and rhetoric;
- check your work and correct it as necessary.

SCORE

1 Here, you have a typical mark scheme. Use a 'best-fit' approach to decide exactly the mark you deserve. (20)

Marks	Descriptors
0–4	● Show the topic is understood ● Some understanding and personal view ● Limited vocabulary ● Some accuracy in spelling and sentences
5–8	● Some analysis though views may seem biased ● Comments on attitudes of young ● Beginning to use discourse markers ● Some variety in sentences and attempts paragraphs ● Much is accurate, with standard English used
9–12	● Shows clarity of thought – a reasoned response with analysis and comment ● Suitably formal and engages the reader's interest ● Uses devices like rhetorical questions, lists, etc. ● Paragraphed well and a range of sentences ● Mostly accurate spelling and punctuation
13–16	● Detailed analysis leading clearly to comments made ● Some subtlety in the way ideas are presented ● Language used effectively: a range of discourse markers and devices ● Paragraphs linked; a wide range of sentences ● Accurate spelling and punctuation
17–20	● Developed analysis, with linked points which support each other, and convincing comment ● Manipulates the reader to agree with the comments ● Complex grammatical structures, used effectively ● Paragraphs appropriate to support the meaning; control of complex sentences ● accurate ambitious vocabulary and punctuation

You can only do your best to fit your work into this framework. However, this allows you to see how skills are rewarded at different levels, and how examiners arrive at your mark. As you improve the elements referred to in this marking grid, you know your final grade will be getting better!

TOTAL

Before the exam

- Make sure you know which paper you will be taking and when.
- Check that you know exactly what each paper is testing.
- Re-familiarise yourself will all pre-release material.
- Revise the skills you will need to display; practise dealing with media and non-fiction texts, responding to questions on poetry and writing in particular genres, as appropriate.
- As well as using this book for last-minute hints and practice, set yourself tasks and respond to them under timed conditions, so that you are well-prepared for the examination itself.

Practise writing to the time limits of the exam.

In the exam

Read the instructions on the paper carefully. You should:

- establish **how many** questions you have to answer overall, whether some need to come from certain sections, whether there are choices within questions, etc.;
- work out **how long** to spend on each question. Apportion time to each question in relation to the marks it carries – in other words, spend twice as long on a question worth 10 marks than on one worth 5 marks.
- check **which text(s) or part(s) of text(s)** you need to use in answering reading questions;
- remember that you can use information provided elsewhere on the paper when responding to writing questions, but you must not simply copy it: put it into your own words and use it for your own purposes.

Questions to test reading

- Do not simply write everything you know about the text. You will only be rewarded for answering the question that has been set.

Read each question carefully so that you can:

- understand exactly what is required, looking at key words such as 'How?' or 'Why?' Underline key words so that you remember to address them in your answer.
- add annotations to the reading material, to help when you write your answer;
- use any prompts to help you focus and structure your answer – try to respond to all of them, otherwise marks may be lost;
- remain focused on the question. Refer to it in your answer and ensure that all you write is relevant.

Media and non-fiction texts

- Do not panic when faced with previously unseen material: work through it quickly, to identify the subject matter and how it is handled.
- You may not have to deal with it all: check on the question(s) and re-read the text(s) with the questions in mind.
- Respond in as much detail as possible, but analyse the material; don't just describe what is there.

Poetry

- If the question asks you to compare, remember to write about two poems. If you do not, you will be limiting the grade you can receive.
- The examiner expects you to comment on the language and form of the poems, as well as the content.
- Include quotations, and analyse their effect.
- Remember the most basic technique: point – quotation – explanation.

Avoiding common mistakes (all types of reading)

- Keep to the subject – don't twist a question to fit something you had prepared earlier.
- Keep narratives simple and explanations relevant and logical – don't try to be too clever.
- Make sure your tone is appropriate – don't ever forget the audience.

Questions to test writing

Writing to argue, persuade, advise

- Structure your response so that the reader can follow your ideas.
- Use a range of techniques: rhetoric, examples, anecdotes, quotations, humour, etc.
- Move to a logical conclusion.

Writing to inform, explain, describe

- Make sure you are doing what the question demands. Remember that information, explanation and description are different.
- Organise your writing sensibly, use appropriate detail and try to support a clear viewpoint.
- Avoid simply listing ideas: develop them and try to relate them, within the response and to the requirements of the question.

Writing to analyse, review, comment

- Avoid random statements: try to analyse and then comment.
- Comments should arise logically from the details you have identified.
- Prove what you believe.

Avoiding common mistakes (all types of writing)

- Concentrate on the given purpose and audience – don't twist a question to fit something you prepared earlier.
- Don't panic and fail to show what you can do. Within the structure you plan, try to show the examiner the skills you have learnt: vary sentences, punctuation and paragraphs, and use techniques like anecdote and rhetoric, and imagery to bring your ideas to life.
- Always check your work carefully at the end. Correct and improve it and collect higher marks.

All types of writing

Make sure that you:

- know exactly what is required in your answer;
- plan your response in as much detail as possible, to properly present and support your ideas;
- pay particular attention to your introduction and conclusion;
- write at your normal speed, taking care over accuracy and legibility;
- concentrate on spelling, punctuation, expression and paragraphing;
- make sure your ideas are linked effectively and your response flows logically;
- constantly think about purpose and audience: are you presenting the right material in the right kind of way?

Planning answers

Although time is so tight, try to plan answers whenever possible – especially in answer to questions testing your writing skills.

- Don't rush into the actual answer until you have got a good idea of what you want to say.
- Decide on the overall structure of your answer, so it is logical and coherent.
- Decide on the best information to use.

Checking

Check your final answer. Have you:

- expressed yourself clearly, with accurate spelling and punctuation?
- set out quotations clearly and accurately?
- included all the material you planned to use?
- ended with a firm conclusion which refers back to the question?

SCORE CHART (1)

Topic	*Check yourself*	Points out of 20
Media texts	1	
Types of non-fiction texts	2	
Fact and opinion	3	
Following an argument	4	
Structure in non-fiction/media texts	5	
Presentational devices	6	
Use of language	7	
Comparing texts	8	
Reading poetry	9	
Reading poetry	10	
Poems from different cultures and traditions	11	
Poetry anthology for AQA/A	12	
Poetry for AQA/B	13	
Spelling	14	
Punctuation	15	
Vocabulary and style	16	
Sentence structures	17	
Structuring whole texts	18	
Presenting written work	19	
Writing to argue	20	
Writing to argue	21	
Writing to persuade	22	
Writing to advise	23	
Writing to inform, explain, describe	24	
Writing to inform, explain, describe	25	
Writing to analyse, review, comment	26	
Writing to analyse, review, comment	27	

SCORE CHART (2)

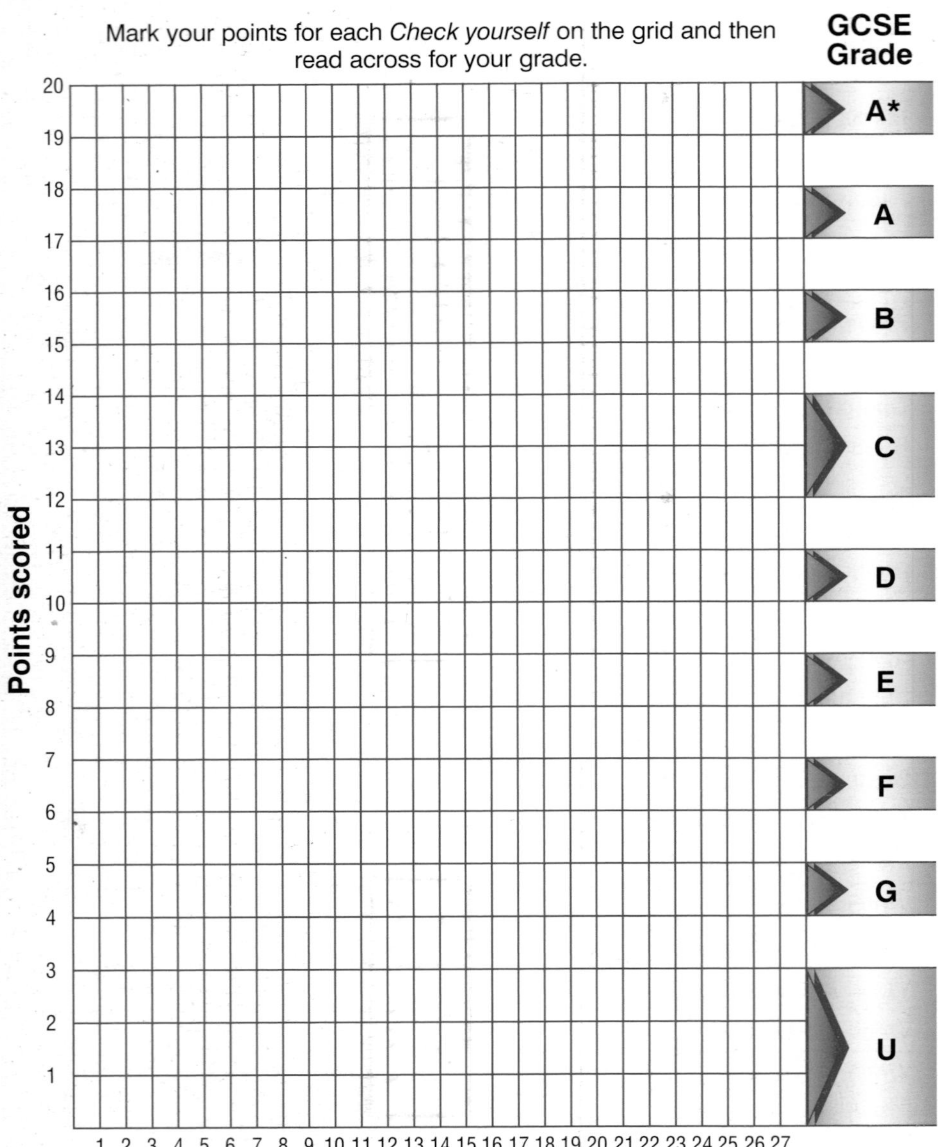